Defenders of Men

For Diane

DK Sanders

Defenders of Men

DONALD K SANDERS

ISBN-13: 9781514391297
ISBN-10: 1514391295
Library of Congress Control Number: 2015912464
CreateSpace Independent Publishing Platform
North Charleston, South Carolina

ALEXEIN ANER or DEFENDERS OF MEN

Not long ago I looked into the meaning of my last name, Sanders. As I was reading the definition, everything became clear to me. It was only one paragraph, but it defines exactly who I am and who my ancestors were for as far back as I am aware of. The male members of the Sanders family have all been military men, including myself and my two brothers, Tony and Mike. My paternal grandfather died before my birth in 1948, but I was told that late in his life he suffered greatly, his lungs burnt by mustard gas in the fields of France during WWI. My father and his brother both served in WWII. My father was stationed at Pearl Harbor when the war began on December 7, 1941. He was sixteen years old. He served in the Pacific on many of the assaults on islands held by the Japanese. He eventually went insane.

My time in the military was spent in Vietnam from June 1969 to August 1971. I have been sour on the idea of my family having to sacrifice so much, generation after generation, for such a little idea as war. I have been very angry for many years. Until lately, I could not identify myself with the actions I committed in the name of God and country. I just couldn't understand it. I struggle with it still.

The name Sanders is derived from the name Sander, or Zander, of medieval England and Germany. To go back further, Zander comes from the Greek word *Alexander* or *Alexandros*. *Alexandros* comes from the combination of two older and more ancient Greek words, *Alexein*, meaning "to defend or help" and *aner* which means "man or men." The surname Sanders literally means "defender of men."

For my wife

Contents

One

The first time I can remember meeting my father was at an airport somewhere in Tennessee when I was very young. I can remember my mother taking my picture on that very day as I was standing near a chain-link fence, watching the airplanes come and go. I wondered which plane he was on. As we waited my mother issued instructions about the dos and don'ts of how we were to act around my father. She spoke of how my father's moods sometimes shifted quickly from happy to sad and then just as quickly to anger, or even rage.

"It was because of the war," she said. "It was very hard on your father, and now his heart is broken just like the shell on an egg."

I listened as she spoke of terrible battles that no human being should have to endure, battles where my father was wounded. He was hurt badly, on the inside as well as the outside. She explained that the illness suffered by my father was nothing for us to be ashamed of because he had been very brave in battle and was awarded many medals for valor, such as the Purple Heart, the Bronze Star, and the Pearl Harbor Medal.

As I stood by the fence, I couldn't remember if I had ever met my father. My mother had to point him out to me as we watched him approach. I found that he was a handsome man of about six feet tall, with a very slim but fit body. I liked the way he carried himself in his military manner, and I remember wishing that someday I would look just like him. I could see the joy in his eyes as he drew nearer, and then there were tears and cries of joy, and there were hugs and kisses for all. It was a happy day. The first day of my memory is happy one.

In the days that followed, I didn't see much of my father, for he hid himself in the bedroom most of the time. My mother and my older brother, Tony, were the only ones allowed inside his secluded refuge, which he kept dark, with the shades drawn. I began to feel shunned, as if somehow my father didn't love me or want me around. It seemed that my younger brother, Mike, and I received only insults and rejection. We were often warned, "Stay away," while he kept Tony close by his side for days on end, loving him and holding him. I could only catch glimpses of them when my mother took them their meals, always served in the bedroom, in private. "Things will get better," my mother promised. It was during these days, while Mike and I were alone for long periods of time with my mother, that I learned much of what I know about my family, past and present. Having my mother's full attention, I began to ask questions, as children often will. These days of my father's isolation were probably some of the most important days of my life, for without them I would know nothing of my ancestry or what had happened in the past that brought me to where I am. I found out that my father was born in the early 1920s in Tennessee, near Murfreesboro. His father was an engineer who had resided somewhere in Ohio. He had served as an officer in the US Army during World War I and had suffered lung damage from the inhalation of mustard gas. My great uncle was a politician and a staunch supporter of Harry Truman.

On my mother's side of the family, my great-grandmother was the daughter of early pioneers. Her parents were poor dirt farmers somewhere in rural Arkansas, where she was born and raised. She had married at a very young age to a man named Roe and thus became Vennie Roe. Her husband died early in their married life in some sort of farming accident, leaving Vennie to fend for herself. Young, inexperienced, and alone on the prairie, she lived in a one-room shack with dirt floors and a broken front door. Later, Vennie is said to have met and set up house with a full-blooded Cherokee Indian, a man of questionable character. They spent the rest of their days on the little homestead, where she bore him several children, among them, my grandmother. Vennie and her man, along with their half-breed children, lived in relative poverty and were considered white trash by many of the community's more upstanding citizens. This fact didn't bother me at all because I was delighted to find that I had the blood of the Cherokee Nation running throughout my veins. Her daughter, my grandmother, married a blacksmith that owned a shop in Humphrey, Arkansas.

I can remember them vividly. She was small, frail, and sickly looking, while he was a huge man with ghostlike white hair and a peaceful look about him that made me always want to be near him. I can remember his huge, strong hands and his white hair that always needed cutting. His hair always hung over his left eye, bouncing, as he worked in his shop. I remember that he would always hold my hand as we walked to his blacksmith shop through the little town of Humphrey. At that time, Humphrey still had sidewalks of wood, which seemed right out of the early cowboy days. On our treks through town, he would greet everyone we met and each and every person we passed knew him by his first name. One and all seemed pleased to see him. To me he was a wonderful gentle giant that was strong enough to bend steel bars with his bare hands, even as old as he was. His whole adult life was spent bent over in his little shop working at his forge, repairing farm equipment for the locals, who would pay little or nothing for his labor, for they also were dirt poor. Often I would pump the bellows, holding up my arm to block the heat, and watch him work at his red-hot forge. Beating the hot metal into shape with his big hammer (which was too heavy for me to lift) made a *clang, clang, clang* noise every time it slammed down on the heated metal. I'd watch him beat the big fat pieces of iron into long flat ones or turn them into a spoon or a heavy shovel. I was always amazed at the ease in which he did these things. It was not until many years after his death that I learned that, at the time when we walked together through the small town, he held my hand because he was nearly blind. All those years working at the forge had robbed him of his sight, and I didn't even know it, for he never mentioned it. I never noticed his failing sight because I was too busy copying his every action. There was no hiding the fact that I wanted to be just like him when I grew up. He was one of the few people I had to look up too; he was a hero to me then and he still is now, to this very day.

My grandmother, though old and feeble, was a seamstress. She made and repaired clothing for local women who would have nothing to do with her socially. A large quilt loom filled her parlor, and she would sit at it for hours. Her feeble, knobby fingers pushed the needle in and out, over and over, day after day, year after year. I can remember the loom well and the beautiful quilts that she would make on it. When not working on it, she would pull it up to the ceiling with ropes and little pulleys. Sometimes when it was up near the ceiling, I would lie on my back and look up at it. Even though it was six or so feet above me, it seemed to keep me warm. I have never been warm like that since. A sewing machine with foot pedals, a wooden work chair, two wooden rocking chairs, and a large old radio were all the furniture that they had in the living room. Their house was in ill repair, with no indoor plumbing except for the water pump at the kitchen sink. A pipe ran from the sink through the wall, and the excess water flowed out of the side of the house into what we called the swamp. It was always muddy and always had its own unique odor.

Just as the sun was about to rise, my grandmother would serve breakfast and my grandfather and I would sit and sip hot coffee from saucers with a loud slurp. He would put extra sugar in the cup that he would offer me. There was very seldom any conversation between my grandparents and it seemed all but natural to me at the time. I had the feeling that they loved each other, talk or no talk.

Together they would have nine children, the first of whom (named after Vennie Roe) died in the year of her birth. Of the nine, I can remember meeting only five. Ray, the oldest son, went to the war in Europe. From D-Day right on through until the Germans surrendered, he fought. I can remember playing with his war trophies, a Nazi flag, a helmet, and a dagger with a swastika engraved upon it. I can vaguely remember meeting him only once, but I remember how proud of him I was then. The youngest son, my uncle Carlee, married once, divorced, and had no children. He worked as a warehouseman in Peoria, Illinois, when we met. I knew my uncle Carlee well, and I was quite fond of him. He told me that Uncle Ray was an alcoholic and suffered from mental problems due in part to his military service. Uncle Ray was also wounded in action somewhere in France and was decorated for valor. I learned many years later that they had both retired somewhere in Florida and died in quick succession. I always fancied that they lie together in some Floridian graveyard, under some peaceful trees on a hilltop, overlooking the rest of the cemetery, with the ocean beyond. I wish I had known them better.

I remember two of my aunts. Aunt Louise was considered the black sheep of the family because she had married a black man. She was never talked about and rarely came to visit her parents. When she did, her husband and their children would wait by the car, outside of the driveway, and slightly out of sight. I can remember meeting her only once or twice. She was surrounded by three or four little half black and half white children that I never got to talk with because they were kept at a distance. I knew that they were my cousins but that I would probably never meet them, and never did. I would love to have the chance to meet them if I could find them. I want to meet their children and the rest of their extended family. I would like to tell them that I love them very much. Lastly, I would like to know where my aunt Louise is and how to contact her.

The oldest daughter, my aunt Inez, was a loving person who married a farmer named Henry Bradshaw. I lived with them for a short time on their little dirt farm. I was always afraid of Uncle Henry, for I don't think that he cared much for the idea of having to support three nephews, even though we worked very hard in his fields after school and on weekends in an effort to please him. It seemed to me, as I think back, that he hit and cursed me for reasons that I never knew. I think that it must have been out of frustration that he had to do, as he would put it, "niggers' work." Another thing that I can vaguely remember is that he always referred to my father as a Yankee, and he seemed upset that my mother would marry one. He and Aunt Inez would have four children, Bobby, Nancy, Joe Donald, and Jimmy. Uncle Henry was a hard man and an avid member of the local KKK, with established bragging rights. He made no secret of his hatred of the black man. When I say he was a mean man, it is because of the things that I saw him say and do to people of color. It was impossible for him to pass, either on foot or in his old rickety truck, without making some sort of racial statement. I felt so sorry for him. His soul was in the possession of the devil. This was clear to me, and I was only about seven years old. I had, by this time, extensive experience in dealing with and recognizing the devil and his doings. The white people he passed on the roads and in the town all seemed to avoid him, and I think that they too could sense the nearness of the devil in him. Life on Uncle Henry's little farm was hard for me and my brothers. Uncle Henry was very abusive in nature, and it was common for me to have to cut my own switch for the whipping he gave me for just about everything that I did or did not do. So it seemed at the time.

His oldest son, Bobby, already a grown man by this time, had moved out and away from his father. His daughter, Nancy, was a senior in high school. Nancy had a gentle nature, and I can only remember how fond of her I was. I can remember little else about her except how submissive she was around her father.

Uncle Henry was a sharecropper and worked the little farm, which was owned by someone else who took half of whatever profit could be derived from his labors. Uncle Henry walked into the built-on bedroom where Tony, Mike, Jimmy, Joe Donald, and I slept. When he heard the language we were using, that was to be the end of our stay with Uncle Henry and Aunt Inez.

My mother was the youngest of the nine. She was born with a wandering eye that was corrected in her early twenties. She was a beauty, with raving black hair and a full bosom. She would attend the one-room schoolhouse, just like her brothers and sisters, but she would be the only one to complete high school. After graduation, she took a job in Little Rock, where she fell in love with my father after meeting at a dance and married him shortly thereafter.

These few stories, and the ones that follow, are all that I know about my family. I wish I knew more, but I don't. The memory of the things that my mother told me that day still linger in my mind, and at many times during my life, these memories were the only things that carried me through the hard times that came so very often.

Just as the time alone with my mother began, it ended. The situation at home worsened. My father's mental health did not improve, and in fact it grew worse. My mother tried to explain away his cruel behavior with excuses and war stories about how he had been terribly wounded in action and had been given the drug morphine to kill the pain. An addiction to morphine was the result. I later found that this was common to soldiers injured in the last few wars. He was awarded two Purple Hearts for his wounds. He received two Bronze Stars for heroic actions in New Guinea, the ancient home of cannibals, with jungles so thick they were impenetrable. There were insects there that would swarm over your body in search of salt. The swarm, by the thousands, would invade every crack and crevice of your body in search of the precious salt until you were driven insane. The combat stress, the wounds he received in action, the addiction to morphine, and the insects I'm sure would drive any normal man insane. Insanity overtook him, and so began of the end of our little family.

His behavior became more and more aggressive, and his anger always seemed directed at Mike and me. A snarl, a curse, and a bombardment of flying objects were all that we would receive from him. Tony was adored and loved with a tenderness that was a kind of worship, as a man would love and adore his god. The Son of God—Tony was the Son of God. Tony was the new messiah, come to save us all. Tony was to be protected at all times from the evil ones; he therefore was kept at my father's side at all times. The looks I got from my father were looks of hate and disgust, a silent warning to stay far away from Tony. For the first time, I felt something new, something that would always remain in my being. *Fear.* I was afraid to go near my father. My mother tried to explain it away, but there was no mistaking it: my father hated me. I was sure that he wanted to kill me and would do so without blinking, just as he had killed all those Japanese during the war. I began to have nightmares of him cutting my head or hands off. With more and more frequency, I would wake in a sweat, crying for my mother, who could not come, for she was in the room with them. My father seemed to loom above me all the time, hunting me, forever stalking, with death in his eye. I was afraid for my life, and I was only six years old.

On one of the worst days of my short life, I could see my father sitting on the bed, holding Tony in his arms, loving him. He had a peaceful look in his eyes, and knowing that I shouldn't, I took the chance and approached him. Asking quietly if I could come in, I slowly crept through the door. When I got close enough, he kicked me hard in the chest. The force of the kick thrust me across the room into the doorjamb, knocking the wind from my little body. I tried to get up, gasping for air like a fish out of water. He was instantly on me. I tried desperately to get away, but without wind I could not scream, just like in my dreams. He grabbed me by the leg with his strong hands. He dragged me out of the room by my leg to the little kitchen. He swung me around and released me, and I flew across the room to where my mother stood doing the dishes. My face slammed against the edge of the sink. I hit hard. I could feel my jaw crack, and I could see my blood, my Cherokee blood, spewing from my face onto the floor and sink. I thought it was the end for me, and I can remember trying to talk to God. My mother was there like a shot. She scooped me up, and just like that we were headed for the stairs. All at once there was yelling and fighting and running and pain, but the thing I remember most was the fear. I cannot explain it nor have I felt such fear since. I was terrified. I knew that I was going to die and that then he would go after Mike. Although I could not see Mike, I could sense his fear, and it was a dread like no other. I feared that I might have to see my brother die. This sent a twinge of anger through my body, but the fear was stronger.

Held tightly in my mother's arms, I could see the walls rushing by. I heard the *clump, clump, clump* of her shoes on the noisy wooden stairs. Then all of a sudden the clump sound changed to a *clack, clack, clack*, and we were in the open air. I saw the people, lots of them, and the looks on their faces. The fear on their faces showed like the sun and kept them from moving. I think that they wanted to help me but were afraid to get involved, frozen in their tracks. My mother was screaming for help at the top of her lungs as she ran. Once in a while, I would catch a glimpse of my father close behind, chasing us with rage and hate in his eyes. To him I was a demon, an evil being that must be destroyed at all cost. He was insane. It was obvious to all that observed these events that he was not to be trifled with, unless you wanted to risk your life to save mine. Only my mother stood firm against a war-hardened killer with a one-track mind. Kill the demon, kill. More and more faces appeared and disappeared as we ran down the street. I could taste the blood in my mouth and saw that my mother's shoulder was covered with it. I can remember how beautiful it looked with its wetness on her shoulder. Finally, we crashed through a door and into a crowded bar. I remember the smell of wet cigarettes and beer. I can remember the looks on their faces as the crowd parted to let us pass: fear, disbelief, and amazement. Some were too busy to care as my father finally reached us, and with a thud that knocked the wind from me, we crashed to the floor, me on the bottom, under the body of my protecting mother, and my ugly, insane father clawing at my arm, wrenching, and trying to pull it out of the socket. I could see the look on his face, and I'll never forget it. I have never seen that look from anyone since; however, I now know that I now have the same look when I'm angry. Then like a blessing from God, I passed out, and I did not witness the arrival of the police and the blood flying all about as both my father and mother were brutally beaten into submission and then unconsciousness by a big policeman with a club. He had no idea who was attacking who or what was going on, but he had to put a quick end to it, and he did.

Sometime later I awoke with a start and found myself in a white hospital bed with my mother's bruised and battered face looking down on me. I remember thinking that she looked like an angel from heaven. My jaw was wired shut but was numb to pain, and my chin had required forty-four stitches to close, but I was alive. I was given melted ice cream so I could drink it through a straw. I didn't notice that my arm was black until I was given a pad and pencil in order to communicate with my mother. It was so sore that I could not use it to write, but I did quite well with my left arm. I can remember vividly the first thing that I wrote. It read, "Am I ugly?" My mother cried as she read it and shook her head. I could see that it hurt her neck as she moved her head to and fro. I napped a lot for a while, and I remember this because every time I went to sleep, I would have a nightmare and wet myself and the bed. I can remember how often I had to be moved in order to change the sheets. It seemed I was always lying in a pool of blood because the urine was full of it, causing a weird reddish color as it stained the sheets. I would soon get used to this because it continued for months.

Sensing my fear, my mother assured me that my father could not bother me ever again. She said that he was in a jail for sick people and that he could not get out. As it turned out, he was committed into an asylum for the criminally insane where he would spend many years of his life. That was the last time I ever saw or heard from my father.

I was still very afraid that he would find me and come to kill me. I remember how much I cried because I knew that, were I in trouble, no one would help me except my mother. I was worried that she would not have the strength to keep him away by herself, and I began to have sleeping problems. I developed ways to awaken myself should someone come for me. Someone approaching would kick a carefully placed object or a crispy candy wrapper, and this would wake me up with a start, a scream, and if I had time, I could make for the door. I was found several times hiding under the bed or behind the door. I would grow so exhausted that when I did sleep, I found myself trying to hide in my dreams. I would be so afraid that I would wet myself, waking in a reddish, wet bed. I began to believe that I would always be afraid, and as it turned out, I was for many, many years.

I would show this fear in many different ways. Sometimes I would tie a string to the doorknob so that if it opened it would awaken me, but this only worked if the door opened the right direction. If the door opened to the inside, I placed something—anything—that would make noise when pushed over. A glass with pennies inside seemed to work the best, and the nurses always kept plenty of pennies on the table by the bed for me. I liked the feeling of being protected while in the hospital because it seemed as if someone was always around, night or day, to watch over me. Sometimes when the nurses heard me screaming, they would come in and change my sheets, often several times a night. This I took as pure acts of kindness and love, something that I would not receive even from my closest relatives.

Within a year, I was living in Humphrey, Arkansas, first with my granny and granddad Fisher, as I called them. They were already in their eighties by this time, and it was all they could do to manage caring for three young grandsons. My mother had simply disappeared, and I was told that she was working in Little Rock and that she would come to see us when she could. I enjoyed living there, in their little farmhouse, surrounded by cotton fields on all sides and a canal that flowed by on one corner. The canal was a place of infinite pleasure for me because I could hide in the berry bushes and play with the crawdads and garter snakes. A giant elm tree stood in the front yard and provided plenty of shade in the heat of the summer. Climbing it led to another place that I felt safe, and I always took a pocketful of rocks with me whenever I perched myself within it.

The house had no indoor plumbing, as I mentioned, except for a hand pump for water in the kitchen that drained out into the swamp, as we called it. The ducks and chickens always hung out at the swamp to eat all the bugs that resided there. The window over the sink was always kept closed to avoid the smell of the swamp, and it was pretty bad too. My brother Mike always seemed to end up covered with swamp mud because the ducks liked to chase him, scaring the hell out of him with their infernal squawking and squealing. Mike always fell for their trap as they chased him around the house, and he inevitably ended up lying face down in the swamp. A one-hole outhouse stood about fifty feet behind the house, and that smell added to the smell of the swamp was pretty bad, but it didn't seem to bother the host of wasps that resided inside. I always hated and feared using the outhouse, not because of the wasps but because I was trapped inside and could not see if anyone was waiting for me outside the door. At night my grandmother would pee in a large ceramic pot, with a cover, neatly tucked under her side of the bed. The boys would just pee off the porch at night and in the bushes during the day, a habit that had a direct influence on the aroma of the little three-room shack.

My grandparents were very kind but showed little affection for us in their daily labors. I cannot remember ever being hugged by my grandmother. My grandfather seemed warmer and I liked to hang out with him when he'd let me. My brothers and I slept on blankets spread on the floor around the large radio that was the major piece of furniture. Except for a few dusty pictures on the wall, there was nothing else in the room but two bentwood rocking chairs with pillowed seats, my grandmother's loom that she pulled to the ceiling with ropes when not in use, and the sewing machine. A coffee can sat on the floor by each rocker, which my grandparents used to spit out their snuff that always filled their mouths. The smell of chewed snuff always stood above all other scents in the house and on their persons.

In the fall, when school started, I attended the same one-room schoolhouse that my mother had attended when she was my age, and everything was still exactly the same except for the recently built two-story brick high school next door. Every morning I would eat breakfast with my grandfather, and we would sip hot coffee from saucers without saying a word. We must have looked kind of scruffy to the other kids because I don't think we had more than two changes of clothes, and they were dirty most of the time since doing the laundry by hand was such a chore for my elderly granny.

A boy named Philip Bates was my only friend at school, but we seldom played together after school, even though he lived only a quarter mile away. Philip was a bully, and I was the only one that got along with him because I was not afraid of him, and he knew it. With the cooperation of the girl down the street, he and I saw our first naked girl, under the school in the crawl space. The only problem with that was when she told her father about it, and I received the first of two whippings that my granddad ever had to give me. I didn't care much for school, and this reflected in my grades. I was not popular with the teacher, and I can remember being sent home several times because I stunk of the odor of urine, which drew complaints from my fellow students.

My mother arrived for a short visit at Christmastime but arguments ensued between her and my grandparents that ruined the holiday, and she left again, this time in tears. I overheard comments about how much longer she expected them to raise her kids and how hard it was to care for us, as old as they were. It was agreed that they would speak with Uncle Henry about whether he would take us in. This I dreaded, because I did not like Uncle Henry at all. As I mentioned before, he was the meanest person whom I had ever met. Because he sensed in me that I did not like what I saw and what was said about "niggers," I was grouped right along with them in his mind.

My mother said that she worked on a stamping machine in a cigarette factory, and that she would not be able to support us for quite some time, so I began to accept the fact that I was bound to have to live at Uncle Henry's sooner or later. Uncle Henry was a dirt-poor sharecropper, working someone else's land for a share in the profits. They existed completely on what the little farm would provide, which wasn't much. The farmhouse was nothing more than a three-room shack, one bedroom separated from a large kitchen and an indoor bathroom. My aunt Inez was a great one for discipline, and it was enforced by my uncle's heavy hand. His word was the law, and to him we were nothing more than small farm hands, good only for working in the fields. He thought school was a waste of time, and he saw it as taking money right out of his pocket. After school my older brother Tony and I worked in the fields alongside the black laborers that took us in hand and showed us how to work at a pace that would conserve our energy so that the long hours of labor would not be so hard on us. I distinctly remember Uncle Henry screaming and ranting and raving at me for taking a drink from a bottle after a black man had taken a drink from it. He slapped me so hard that a crooked tooth punched through my cheek, cracking the tooth, which later broke in half.

Their youngest children, Joe Donald and Jimmy, had dropped out of school in favor of farm work during their early teens. Their daily routine was twelve hours' hard labor working the fields by hand because there was a complete lack of farm equipment. Every day after walking the three or so miles from the school to the farm, my brothers and I would join the laborers in the fields until dinnertime, which was served at dusk. A large table was the gathering place for dinner and we always said prayers before meals, but I always felt as if Uncle Henry was praying to the devil. Later we would sit circled around an old radio listening to *The Lone Ranger* or *Flash Gordon* before bedtime. Joe Donald also had a strange fascination with animals that I think may be common among boys raised on farms. Otherwise, I got along with them fine as long as I could avoid my uncle's heavy hand. Like I said, he enjoyed making me cut and fetch my own switch, which he used liberally for any reason he could find. I think that he and Joe Donald had the same perverted personality.

Several trips to the hospital were the only occasions that gave me a break in my dreaded routine. Once I received some stitches for a cut I gave myself with a garden hoe, and another time after a bee sting I was again rushed to the emergency room, barely breathing and swollen beyond recognition. The school-and-work routine continued until the end of the school year, and on the last day of school, I was called aside and told that I had failed to pass the third grade and that I would have to repeat it again next year. My brothers, Tony and Mike, had also failed the first and fifth grades, and we were the only students in the whole school system that had failed to pass. After school, we walked the three miles to Uncle Henry's in a sad silence that was broken only by the jeers and jokes of the other kids that followed as we walked. As we neared the farm, I saw my mother standing there waiting in the yard for us.

Tony and Mike ran to greet her. Slowly, I approached her and she asked, "Did you pass third grade for me?" I replied no and began to cry, which earned me a big, loving hug, something that was unfamiliar to me, evidenced as I stood there tautly.

The next morning, Uncle Henry drove us all to Granny and Granddads, where we ate a big breakfast and talked until a man in a strange car arrived, and I and my brothers were loaded into the backseat. As we were driving away, I looked out the back window to see my grandmother and my aunt Inez crying and waving good-bye. My mother smugly told us that they were not real tears but crocodile tears. When I asked, "Where are we going?" my mother told us that we were going to Little Rock to help some friends harvest their pear crop.

After our arrival at our destination, we slept on the floor in a strange farmhouse. We were awakened early, fed, and trucked to an orchard where we spent the day picking and eating pears. I enjoyed working with and helping the black laborers, who always treated me better than my own relatives, and besides, I was with my mother. That evening after dinner, we returned to the same floor for another night, rudely interrupted after I wet myself and my brother Mike. Mike was angry, but I understood because I had just peed all over him. The next morning after breakfast, we again loaded into the strange man's car and drove away from the pear farm, never to return.

Two

The strange man in the strange car drove us into Little Rock. I remember thinking that it was a dirty town. The strange man drove in silence, turning this way and that all morning until we passed through a large metal gate. In an arch, the words *St. Joseph's Home* towered well over our heads. At first I thought it was just a nice park, until I saw it. Looming there, like something out of a Boris Karloff movie, stood a huge, dark building with windows made up of little squares. Swirling above the building was a black circle that seemed to be moving. I watched it closely as we got closer, and it turned out to be hundreds of dark birds circling around and around like a dark tornado. My eyes followed the birds as they disappeared behind a tall smokestack and then reappeared on its other side.

Farther away my eyes found a fence that was almost hidden from view by green vines that climbed up to its top and draped over like a dark curtain. Standing, as far as I could tell, about eight feet tall, it appeared to enclose the entire park. I wondered if they wanted to keep someone out or if they wanted to keep someone in. It was at that moment that I knew something was very wrong, that something was going to happen, but I didn't know what. As we approached, the building grew larger and larger, and the birds became louder and louder, and I looked at my mother to see if she had seen them. I almost said something to her but something held me back because I knew she had been upset all morning about something.

Two tall, dark, intricately carved wooden doors began to open as if in slow motion until at a certain point I saw something strange. A person, a woman dressed all in black was followed quickly by several other dark figures, each holding the big door for the other. I could feel a knot growing inside me, swelling bigger and bigger until I could hardly breathe. The knot began to choke me, and I thought that the fear would consume me, for I knew, in my heart, that this was an evil place. I was so afraid, and I didn't know what was going to happen, but I knew it was not going to be good.

The man pulled up to the curb in front of the doors and stopped just long enough for my mother to get out of the car and go inside with the dark women. Silently he drove to a small parking lot with no cars, stopped again, and turned off the car. I noticed that he had parked across the parking lines instead of pulling into one space. He gave us a faint smile that somehow seemed so sad. He said that we would wait here for our mother to return, and after about thirty minutes, she did. She looked like she had been crying as she opened the back door and told Mike and I to get out so that we could take a walk and talk for a while. She said, "There's a grotto nearby that we will enjoy seeing. We can sit and talk there." The grotto was like a small cave with statues of Jesus and his mother, Mary, standing at the entrance and the exit. A concrete bench big enough for us all to sit on sat in the shade nearby. Slowly my mother began to talk, her voice so low and quiet that we moved in close to her so we could hear what she was saying. She said that Mike and I would have to stay here for a while. I thought at first that she was joking, but she explained that she could not support us all at home. It was not healthy for us, she said.

She said, "Tony will be staying with me for the meantime." She promised, "I will come and get you boys as soon as I can." Mike began to cry and told her, "I don't want to stay here; I want to go with you." She shook her head and said, "I'm sorry, Mike, but you have to stay here with Keith." She said that there were lots of kids here and that we would like it here when we got used to it. This reasoning didn't seem to help, and Mike began to cry all the louder. A different type of swelling grew inside of me; a swelling that I knew would become a cry if I let it get out. My mother said that there were lots of nuns living here to take care of the children. "You'll like it when you get used to it, won't you, Keith?" she said. I just gave a quick nod, unable talk with the huge lump in my throat that was ever threatening to burst out into tears. My mother also began to sob, while holding us tightly in her arms, until slowly, as if she had become ill, she stood up and we all started to walk toward the big dark building.

Mike began to cry even louder when a lady in a black dress with a black hood on her head stood in the doorway as we approached the ugly building. It was a dreadful sob that soon became a begging wail, so mournful that it sent shivers up my back and shot straight into my heart. It was obvious, so clear, that crying would do no good. We would have to stay. There was no getting around it. It took everything, all the strength that I had, to hold back the tears. I didn't realize it then, but I would become an expert at not crying. Inside the door stood several more of the dark women in their dark dresses, like they were waiting to pounce on us when we entered. They all wore a cross, hanging on a chain, around their necks. Seeing Jesus on the cross made me think of Tony. I wondered why he was the only one to stay with Mom. Maybe he really was someone important to God, just as my father had said. Mike was crying louder now and beginning to beg. "Please, don't leave me," and "Please take me with you," over and over until I thought my head would bust open. It continued to grow to such intensity that my mother began to cry and sob uncontrollably also.

I heard the dark lady, called Sister Conchada, tell my mother that it would be better if she would just leave now. "We will take very good care of your boys," she said. Mike was laying on the floor now, his arms wrapped tightly around my mother's leg. Tears and snot ran all over his face as he screamed, "Don't leave me, don't leave me," but he was pried out of my mother's arms by two of the dark ladies so that my mother could walk freely, out the door, leaving us behind. I watched the scene before me in silence. It was as if I was watching a play in which all the characters wore black and were evil villains. I felt as if someone had reached into my chest and ripped my heart out. I could not speak for fear of behaving just like Mike. This, I would not do. In fact, then and there, I made a promise to myself that I would never cry again, ever. I almost instantly broke that promise as my mother walked through the big wooden door and down the long sidewalk toward the car, where the strange man and Tony waited for her. She never looked around, as I expected her to. I half expected her to walk back in and get us, but she didn't, and then she got into the black car and was gone.

Restrained by two of the dark ladies, Mike was screaming out of control, and all I could do was stand there and watch in disbelief. Silently, I stood beside Sister Conchada, and my heart felt like it was up near my throat. I remember every moment of what had happened that day, and I remember making the statement to the sister that I hadn't cried. She told me that I was a good boy. Things turned to the darker side when the sisters failed to control Mike's crying. They led us down a long hallway, up several flights of stairs, and then down another long hall that was much darker than the first one. Now I began to feel very afraid because they were dragging Mike in a yanking motion that moved him about five feet or so before they had to yank him again. There was no noise, total silence, except the sound of our own footsteps and Michael's crying. I vividly remember my thoughts at that time. I wondered, as we walked down the hall, what had we done that was so terrible. What was forcing my mother to put us in a place like this? I thought that I must be like so much garbage, useless, to be thrown away and not wanted by anyone; no one in our family wanted us. Earlier, downstairs, I had seen a tear in Sister Conchada's eye, but now she was all business, walking so fast that Mike and I now had to run to keep up with her. Looking over at Mike, I could see that he had wet his pants. His pants were wet all the way down one leg. We were taken into a large bathroom with twenty or so sinks on one wall and just as many toilets on the opposite wall. The sister told Mike to strip off his pants and underwear, but Mike could only stand there and sob, looking straight at me as if I could change things. I helped him because he was so very upset, but I struggled with him and could not do it by myself. At this point the sister stepped in and pushed him backward so hard that he bounced onto the floor, screaming all the louder. I began to grow something new inside of me, something that I did not like, but could not stop. This was the first time that I can remember ever wanting to hurt someone. I watched as the sister washed Mike's clothing in a sink, wrung them out, and told him to put them back on. All the while the sister lectured that this and all bathrooms were not to be used and that we had no business at all on the upper floors unless we were told to be there. The ground floor washroom was to be used during the daytime. She stressed that it was always our duty to clean up after ourselves and keep

18

everything clean at all times. "Make a mess, and you will be punished," she told us as we quickly returned to our trek down the dark hallways. She also told us that if we wet ourselves, we would just have to wear wet clothing until laundry day, which came only once a week. We climbed another flight of stairs into another long, dimly lit hallway.

As we walked, the sister spewed out a long list of memorized rules that I could not keep up with and understood only a few. She continued with the words, "The rules are to be followed at all times. Never run in the halls or on the stairs, never wander around, always clean up after yourself, and be absolutely quiet at all times," she said. "Break any of these rules, and you will be punished." She repeated this over and over. On and on and on she went, with rule after rule, until finally we entered a large room filled with row after row of beds. Each bed had a number on it. All were neatly made up, and all had a small pile of what I thought to be pajamas neatly stacked under the top right leg of the beds. Mike was assigned to a bed in the center of the room, while I was given one against the far wall. We were told to stay there and be quiet while she went to get some sheets and blankets for us. Her heavy black shoes *clack, clack, clacked* down the hall until Mike's sobs were the only sound that I could hear. After some time, the sister reached the point in the hallway where the sound of her footsteps softly began to echo, quiet at first, and then louder and louder until I could no longer hear them because she was standing there in front of me. I leaned on one of the beds and held Mike, trying to comfort him and stop his crying. I kept telling him that everything would be OK. This I did not even believe myself. She began spewing out more rules as she demonstrated exactly how our beds were to be made each and every morning and where our clothing and shoes were to be stacked neatly under our beds. Over and over she told us that if we broke the rules we would be punished. I again felt the strange feeling that I wanted to hurt her, but this time the feeling was more intense and closer to the surface.

I noticed that there was a big *US* on the blanket, and it felt rough and scratchy on my skin as I rubbed it with my hand. The sister explained that we had missed dinner but that if we were hungry, she would bring us a snack. "Just this one time," she said. Mike just sobbed and started to hiccup, and with the big lump in my throat, I could only shake my head, indicating that I was not hungry. At that, we were off again, the sister half dragging Mike along as she scurried down the hall.

Far down the hall, and down another dark staircase, we were led into another large room that was filled with children of all shapes and sizes. If I hadn't seen them, I never would have known they were there because they were so quiet. I was not aware of them until we rounded the corner and I could see that all eyes were on us as we entered the room. A hush went down over the already quiet room. The sister told us that we were to stay there and play and meet the other kids until it was time for chapel and then bed. She said that we could play with anything as long as we were quiet at all times. All the children stared directly at us as Mike sobbed and held onto me tightly, afraid to let go. Some of the kids snickered and pointed at Mike's wet clothes. Soon we were being bombarded with questions such as, Are you staying long? Where are you from? How old are you? We gave no answer; I was unable to speak with the big lump in my throat.

I think that my primal survival instincts must have kicked in because I quickly led Mike to the nearest corner. I had hoped to escape the crowd of strange kids. It was to no avail because soon we were encircled by ten or eleven of the biggest kids, who started calling us names, spitting out some of the nastiest words that I had ever heard. That corner is where we stood and waited until we heard a whistle that sent everyone silently scurrying to line up against a wall. I thought about what I had learned in just this one afternoon. First, I was here and I had to deal with it. Second, it doesn't matter where you are, how old you are, or what you are doing, it is always true that in any strange circumstance, it will be the bullies that approach you first. They do not like you, they are not your friends, and they always travel in packs, like wolves. Thirdly, you can try to avoid the bullies, but eventually you will have to deal with them. You can either cower and obey their will or stand and take what they dish out. At that moment, I didn't know what I'd do. There, against the wall, we waited until we were led by the sister to a small room that looked like a narrow church. Two rows of pews were separated by a red carpet running down the center to a marble altar surrounded by statues and red curtains that ran from ceiling to floor. I found that chapel was to be a twice-a-day occurrence, one hour before breakfast and one hour before bedtime. Not wanting to draw attention, we fell in at the end of the line. I found that it was impossible not to be the center of attention because of Mike's constant sobbing. The sobbing drew a loud "Silence!" from the sister, which echoed down the hall and bounced back to us over and over and over. Now I understood the need for silence, because the slightest whisper could be heard clearly from some distance down the hall. I found that chapel, an important daily event, was not an unpleasant experience. The sisters began singing songs in some foreign language, and it sounded like angels singing from heaven. It was so beautiful. Much of the hour was spent on my knees, where I was expected to pray for God to do this or that in the hope of saving my soul, but I had learned and I knew that God didn't like me, so I just kept quiet and said nothing. I felt quite content just to listen to the others as they prayed. Through the following years, it was always the same prayer. Give me this, and I will do that. It made me sick inside. I found that I could tune them all out by trying to remember what my mother's face looked like. It turned out that this was a problem for me all my life. When someone left or died, I always forgot what they looked like. It troubled me at first, but soon I just didn't care anymore and had to think of something new to tune out the prayers of others. Soon my thoughts turned to something new that I could understand: revenge.

After chapel Mike and I fell into the end of the line again. When a hush came over the hallway and spread from person to person all the way down the line, it could only mean that Sister Conchada was approaching. The new quiet brought Mike's sobbing to the forefront again. I tried to quiet him down, but in the end it drew another sharp *"Silence!"* that echoed off the walls with such force that Mike and I could only cower. He held onto me that much tighter there in the dark hall at the end of the line. Mike's sobbing seemed to be at a lower tone, and I hoped that it would stop soon because it was bringing so much attention to us, but as we neared the dormitory, it again seemed to get louder and louder. Once in the dormitory, everybody went to their assigned beds and began to undress, folding their clothes neatly and stacking them at the foot of each bed. Mike was not taking off his clothes, so I went over and helped, folding his damp pants that I noticed still smelled of urine. The smell of urine made me think about my own problem with wetting the bed. I knew that it wouldn't be long before everyone knew that I was a bed wetter. I hoped that I wouldn't but knew that I would.

Mike said that he wanted to sleep with me, but I told him that he couldn't. I told him that I was only a few rows away and promised that I would watch over him and would not let anything happen to him. At the approaching sound of the sister's footsteps, I rushed to my own bed and began to undress. At the sound of a loud clap, the children knelt by their beds and began to say a prayer, but I didn't pray because I was mad at God. The sister flicked the lights out following the prayer and like a ritual, everyone began climbing into bed. There was total silence except for Mike, who's sobbing seemed without end. The sister gave another sharp "Silence!" and clapped her hands loudly before disappearing back into the same shadows from which she had appeared. Her footsteps grew fainter as she walked away down the hall. I listened, hearing only two things. One was the *clack, clack, clack* sound of the sister's footsteps echoing as she walked down the hall, and the other was my brother's sad sobs that were breaking my heart. I lay there listening to him sobbing, sometimes calling my name. This went on for some time until out of the silence came a new sound that I would learn to recognize as the "nasty creepers." The nasty creepers were a gang of young thugs that crept around after the lights were out to either bully or even molest the smaller kids. This was my first encounter with the creepy gang, and it was to teach me a valuable lesson.

My brother was calling my name now, and the low moan of a sob had now grown to a cry of fear and desperation. I knew that this could be heard throughout the dorm, and down the hallway it would echo over and over. The sound of Mike's sobbing carried over the whole room—it drew shushes from the other kids—and suddenly Mike was frantically calling for me. I knew something was wrong. I could see several boys standing around Mike's bed, and it looked like they were pulling his blankets off. When they tried to pull off his underwear, I was on my feet. I went to his bedside, picked up the blanket and put it over Mike, and then stood there like an idiot as one of the boys hit me square in the nose and called me a fucker. He then tore the blanket off again. Seeing blood run from my nose, Mike began to scream louder and louder, which sent the boys scrambling for their beds, leaving me standing alone by Mike's bed. I could hear footsteps coming down the hall, and soon Sister Conchada stood before me, blocking the way back to my bed. "This is a good time for you to learn the rules," she said as she dragged me by the hair down the hall and into a room that was completely covered with little white tiles. Even the ceiling, walls, and several benches were covered by the tile. There was a row of dingy-looking bathtubs with brown stains that ran from the faucets to the drains. A few dirty shower stalls with the same stains and a row of seatless toilets that looked like they had never been cleaned was all that the room contained. As sister Conchada began to speak, I turned to see a wooden paddle hanging on the wall. I could see that there were holes drilled into it. I began to feel afraid again. The sister said, "Drop your underwear," as she reached for the paddle. I stood there naked, embarrassed, and afraid as she spanked me hard, three times. She said, "You will learn to behave and follow the rules." I could hear the echo of other kids as they counted loudly at each whack of the paddle on my bottom. "One, two, three," and then a roar of laughter filled the halls. I would learn later that this was an old custom, and it seemed to me that this was the only fun that anybody ever had in this place. I found that the record number of swats was ten and that this record belonged to some long-forgotten, nameless kid whose only claim to fame was the swat record. I felt like crying, but I knew that if I started, I might not be able to stop. I already had enough problems with Mike and the other kids, so I told myself I would not cry, and I didn't.

The sister told me that she had been kind to me this time because I was new, but the next time the punishment would be severe. "Now go back to your bed and go to sleep" were her final words to me that night, but I knew that there would always be tomorrow. On the way back to my bed, I checked on Mike. He was sucking his thumb, so I knew he was on his way to dreamland. I was grateful for this because I didn't know how much more of it I could take. As I found my bed, I could hear the other kids chuckling and jeering at me. I wanted to go to sleep, but I couldn't. I dreaded the morning.

I was awakened by the glare of bright lights, a loud whistle, and the screeching voice of Sister Conchada yelling, "Everyone get up! Chapel in half an hour; hurry up." One by one, the kids climbed out of bed and began getting dressed. I realized that I was lying in a pool of my own piss, and that I must hide it or I would never live it down, so I slid out of bed, keeping the wet spot covered, and pulled on my pants over my wet underwear. Pants on, I started to make my bed but was told by a fat kid in the next bed not to make it because the bed checker had to check it for pee spots first. Sure enough, I could see the bed checker working his way toward me. The chubby, round-faced kid tried to smile as he told me that if your bed is wet, you must turn in your wet sheets for dry ones and then get in line for swats. "But they don't hurt that bad," he said.

I could see the bed checker getting closer and closer, and there were a few kids stripping their beds, which I was grateful for, because I didn't want to be the only bed wetter. As he drew near, I hoped that he would not find my wet bed, but he was good at his job, and he enjoyed it. Closer and closer he got until he stood by my side and threw the blankets back, exposing the big wet spot. "Strip your sheets and take them to the sister," he said, smiling all the while. As I approached the line, I was happy to see that there were about ten other kids that had wet the bed. I felt a sudden poke in the back and turned to see the chubby kid's smiling face. Two at a time were called into the swat room, with the whole dorm counting each swat. It seemed that the chubby kid was to be my swat partner because we were the last of the bed wetters. The sister didn't seem too happy to see me as she told us to drop our underwear. I caught the chubby kid sneaking a peak at my wiener. He tried to hide it, but it was too late, and I smiled as he received his swats. I received an extra swat because I had not finished dressing; I had forgotten to put on my shoes. "Out," she ordered, and I found the chubby kid waiting for me in the hall.

Together we walked to the big bathroom, where we peed into adjoining urinals and then waited for a sink, where the chubby kid stuck a toothbrush into a yellow box of baking soda and began to brush his teeth. I didn't have a toothbrush, so I just washed my face and ran my finger over my teeth. It was then that I noticed that Mike was nowhere to be found. I rushed off to find him, but he was not in the dorm or the bathroom, and his bed was stripped. I frantically searched everywhere, but I could not find him. "What are you doing?" came the screeching voice, and there was no mistaking who the voice belonged to. I timidly told her that I couldn't find my little brother. The sister grabbed my arm roughly and put me at the end of the line that had formed in the hall. "You had better worry about yourself'" was her only reply. When she noticed that I didn't have my shoes on, she practically threw me back into the dorm and told me to get them on quick because everyone would be late for chapel, and then I would pay dearly. Mike was nowhere to be found, and I wanted to cry again but again refused to do so. It was getting harder and harder not to.

I finally made it to the chapel line just as it began to move, and I did manage to get my shoes on with some considerable effort. Down the long, dark halls and up a flight of stairs we entered the chapel after passing through two large, carved doors. It was truly a beautiful church, with its stained-glass windows depicting the twelve stations of Christ. There were many rows of benches with the fold-down kneelers, and as we entered the room, everyone else was already on their knees and saying their prayers. This was my first morning in the orphanage, and on entering the chapel, I got a feel for exactly how many kids were kept in this place, and there were hundreds of them. I tried to count the rows of benches, but after receiving a cold stare from the sister, I copied everyone else and pretended to pray. As I knelt in the chapel, everyone else praying to God, I told myself for the first time that I must try to forget about my family. I repeated over and over, "Mom is gone, Tony is gone too, but he is God, Mike is gone, Mom is gone." I wondered if I would ever see them again as I chanted my chant that others might have mistaken for a prayer.

After chapel, I was told by the sister to come and see her after breakfast because she had a mess for me to clean up. "Yes, Sister," was my only reply, and I did not ask about my brother, but it was heavy on my mind. As I waited in line for breakfast, the chubby kid worked his way back to stand next to me in line. "He's probably in the little kids' dorm," he said. "Don't worry; you'll see him on the playground sometimes." Instantly I felt better, and I asked him what his name was, and he told me it was Philip Sutter. He said that he was born and raised right here in Little Rock, and that his father was very rich because he owned a big candy company called the Sutter Candy Company.

He said that no one believed it, but it was true. When I asked why he didn't live with his father, I was told that the courts had put him there because his father had done nasty things to him. He thought though that his dad would come and get him someday. When he asked if I had a mom and dad, I told him that I had a mom, but that she had left me there and I didn't know if she was coming back for me or not.

We sat and ate together, and I found that the food was served by the older kids, as they walked around with large pots on a cart and shoveled portions onto each plate. We had powdered milk, powdered eggs, and some kind of white stuff that Philip called mush. This I didn't like, so I gave it to Philip, and he gobbled it up. Philip said that he didn't like it either, but he was hungry and it was all there was to eat. After breakfast I told Philip that I had to go and see the sister and that I expected to get some more swats. He told me to come and find him in the playroom when I was done and we would play some cards. "OK," I said.

When I found the sister, I was given a pail of soapy water and a sponge and told to clean up the spots of blood that had fallen onto the floor the night before when I was given the bloody nose. I was told to clean it up until she returned and to behave myself. Having finished the cleaning, I counted the rows of beds at five rows of ten beds and one row of five. I learned later that only fifty-three were being used, and that there were two other dorms, one for the older kids and one for the younger. There was supposed to be another for babies, but no one I talked to had ever seen it.

On the other side of the big building, there was an identical set up but for girls. No boy was ever permitted to go over to the girl's side. I waited about an hour and a half for the sister to return, but when she didn't, I decided that it was better to wait there all day than to wander around looking for her and risk more punishment. As I waited, I began to chant, "Mom is gone, Tony is gone, Mike is gone." Finally, she appeared with her dark black dress flowing behind her, and there was a mean look on her face. She checked my work and then took me to the playroom. "You had better learn to follow the rules or there will be no end to your problems. I repeated, "Yes, Sister."

I felt very much the center of attention as I entered the playroom and looked for Philip, who was sitting in the corner at a table surrounded by several other kids whom I assumed were friends of his. Philip said that he had saved me a place at the table to play cards. I noticed that Philip was shuffling as old a deck of cards as I had ever seen. I found that the other kids were named Larry, Ed, and Charles. Charles it seems was a little slow, and his voice would drag and stutter as he tried to talk. They asked if I knew how to play crazy eights, and I told them that I had never heard of it. It was easy to learn though, and I was soon playing with the best of them. As we played we asked questions of each other, and Philip seemed to know the most about what was going on because as he said, he had been there for years. Philip said that his mom had died but he still had a dad and that someday he was coming to get him. Larry, Ed, and Charles were full-fledged orphans in that they had no one at all on the outside. Ed said that he had been adopted once but that they had returned him to the home for no reason at all.

I could see the boy who had punched me in the nose, and he and his friends were pointing at us and calling us the pee boys. I looked around and sure enough, everyone at our table had been in the bed wetter line this morning. Philip said not to pay attention to them because the bigger boy named Jim was a bully and liked to beat up everybody. He was the leader of the nasty creepers. Phillip said that Jim was a very nasty boy and that he was always trying to do dirty things to the little kids. I decided to stay away from those boys. Charles told me that I smelled like pee, which embarrassed me. Philip told me that I should do what they do and I wouldn't smell so bad. Philip said that once I get into bed, I should take off my underwear and put them under my pillow, and that way they would be dry and somewhat clean in the morning. I thought that it was a brilliant idea and promised that I would try it. I asked Philip if he had nightmares that caused him to wet the bed, and he said that he just dreams that he gets up and goes to the bathroom, but in reality, he is wetting the bed. Charles thought that was funny and let out a weird sort of chuckle with a snort at the end.

It was a long time before I saw Mike again, but I always had an eye out for him. After a while I began to think that I would never see him again, but I did not cry. Philip and I became fast friends, and we hung out together constantly. I called him Fat Phil and he called me Rocket Don because he said that my wiener looked like a rocket ship. Soon we laughed when the other kids called us the pee boys, and it seemed to annoy them to no end. We were inseparable, and we stuck holes in our fingers with an old nail to draw blood. We became blood brothers by placing our hands together so my Indian blood would mix with his. It seemed the natural thing to do. I really appreciated Fat Phil, my blood brother, because I didn't seem to make many friends, but Phil was all I needed.

We always seemed to find ways to avoid Mean Jim and his fucker friends, as we called them, but one day Jim crept up as we lay in the grass, playing cards. Mean Jim kicked Fat Phil in the balls as hard as he could and then spit on him and ran away laughing. Phil lay there in pain, holding his balls and crying, but for some reason I was on my feet, chasing after Mean Jim. Mean Jim stopped in his tracks, looked at me, and asked, "What are you going to do now?" The smile on his face made me so angry that I kicked him square in the balls, and he was down on the ground, trying to get up. I did not hesitate as I got him into a headlock, threw him back to the ground, and punched him repeatedly in the face. Mean Jim was bleeding profusely from his nose and lips that I split wide open. Mean Jim told me that I had better let him up or he would kick my ass. All of a sudden I had a brilliant idea, all on my own. It was then and there that I realized the power that I had over Mean Jim. I realized that he could not get up unless I chose to let him up. I began to choke him hard, and after a while I could feel him fighting for air, whimpering as if he were dying. I think I would have killed him but for the intervention of one of the older kids who was assigned to supervise the younger kids on the playground. He pulled me off Mean Jim, dragged me into the building to the tiled room, and told me to await Sister Conchada.

"Sister Conchada will take care of you," he said as he left the room, and she did too. He was telling the sister what I had done, and then told her that I had tried to kick him in the balls too when he broke up the fight. I received five hard swats and a lecture before being told to stand with my nose in a corner until dinnertime, which was several hours away. I could hear Fat Phil's voice from the doorway saying, "You're a dangerous man. Nobody's gonna mess with us anymore." And he was right; they didn't. I began to enjoy my newfound power and practiced it on one and all, except for Phil and a few others. I was destined to become the new dorm bully, and I did. It wasn't long before I noticed that the other kids were avoiding me just as they had avoided Mean Jim, who, as a matter of fact, got his ass kicked every time I saw him. Of course the number of swats from the sister was not equal the number of fights, so it seems that I was also destined to become Sister Conchada's biggest discipline problem. I kept thinking that the sister's arm would fall off sooner or later with all the swats that she was giving me, so to be a smartass, I asked her if her arm was getting sore. This was a big mistake because it caused a marked increase in the power that she used, and as a result, the swats were no longer swats; they were beatings. Swats for wetting the bed, swats for fighting, and swats for just about everything I did because I was becoming a very evil little boy. I soon began to enjoy the swats and found myself becoming sexually stimulated as I stood naked before Sister Conchada. The sister noticed it and seemed to swing the paddle even harder as a result. I began to smile at her as she beat me, and it seemed to infuriate her, and I would even count along with the kids in the dorm as they all kept count of my swats. I always felt like a big man when I returned to the dorm after a good beating. Mean Jim would cower in his bed when I passed by, staring at him with my evil eyes. I had become all powerful.

The sister pulled me aside on the day before school was to start and told me that I was to attend school with the other kids in the morning, but in the afternoon I was to go to work in the kitchen. I didn't care much for school, so I didn't mind the kitchen at all. I found that I was the only kid from my dorm to work in the kitchen, and I was the youngest boy there. The sister that was in charge of the cooking crew told me to work with a big boy named Fred, and he showed me what I was supposed to do. He told me that I must be a real troublemaker because no one as young as me had ever had to work in the kitchen. Fred said that the sister had told him to keep me very busy at all times. Of course, being the smallest kid there, I drew the worst jobs, like the daily cleaning of the grease trap, which was the nastiest and messiest job in the kitchen. I was to scrub the pots and pans, the grease trap, and the bathroom twice daily.

Let me tell you about the grease trap. It consisted of a series of little boxes covered by metal grills that were designed to trap anything and everything that should not go down the drains. It was probably the grossest thing that I'd had to do in my life (up to that time). I had to clean out each trap twice daily, by hand. It smelled to high heaven, and at different times, I found everything under the sun, including dead rats, in the traps. I didn't mind the work, but I always seemed to smell of urine and burnt grease, and of course, my new name became trapper boy. I was always glad when laundry day came around, because by the end of the week, my clothes were shiny and stiff from the grease. The sisters always were angry and constantly complained if my clothes were so bad that they had to give me clean ones, which wasn't very often. On laundry day, which occurred once a week, everyone would line up, strip naked, throw the dirty clothes into a pile and wait in line until it was your turn to get clean clothes. This process involved the sister holding up a shirt or some pants next to each kid to see if they might fit. If she decided that any certain article of clothing would fit you, that's what you got, like it or not. I don't think I ever wore the same clothes twice. Sometimes they fit, but ordinarily they didn't. Underwear and socks always had holes in them.

Fat Phil and I ruled the dorm, and with his brain and my brawn, we went a long way. Fat Phil was much smarter than I was so, even though I could beat the holy hell right out of him, he was the leader of the pack. Every dirty trick or deviant scheme that we perpetrated upon our fellow orphans originated inside Fat Phil's little brain. At first Fat Phil and I used our little schemes just to protect ourselves from being molested, but we soon could beat the hell out of all of them, and we did. I admired him; I thought he was a genius. Often I was simply dumbfounded at the brilliance of his ideas. Wonderment filled me as he worked his little mind, and I would sit patiently nearby until I would see that all-too-familiar look on his face that could only mean "brilliant idea coming right up!" Careful planning and plotting, with much discussion of the new plan, would take place in our private area, a far corner in the playroom. My head would touch his head as we sat opposite each other in the dark corner. We could see the other kids talking among themselves and sometimes pointing our way, for they all had become familiar with our nasty little ritual of meanness. I know that they were all thinking that they were the target of our plot, for at one time or another, we had successfully inflicted pain upon them all.

Sometimes we were playful if we liked the kid, but most of the time, our plots were mean and cruel. Nothing was out of bounds. Everything under the sun was available to us, and we usually took it out on the nasty creepers. Fat Phil was truly a genius. I found that he had always been and always would be the ruler of the roost. Even when Mean Jim was the head bully of the dorm and had beat up Fat Phil regularly, Fat Phil had always gotten his revenge. His underhanded plots had wreaked havoc upon the life of poor Mean Jim. Maybe that was why Jim was so mean; he probably knew that Fat Phil was at the bottom of all his misery but had no proof, which forced him to bully anyone that he thought might have been involved in his constant bad luck. Things were stolen from him, lies were told to the sisters about him, and nothing that he cared about was safe. One instance that I particularly admired was when Fat Phil told me that he had placed a turd under Mean Jim's pillow and then watched as he looked around for what was stinking. Fat Phil said that Mean Jim had accused everyone around his bunk of shitting their pants. Fat Phil laughed and laughed while stuffing his face into his pillow, out of sight of Mean Jim. He laughed so hard that he wet the bed before he even fell asleep. This "turding," as he called it, occurred before I had arrived at the orphanage, so Fat Phil suggested that we should do it again so I could enjoy it too. It's true; the sheer brilliance of Fat Phil will never be topped, at least when it comes to evil plots. We turded Mean Jim from then on from time to time, and each and every time, it was the funniest thing that I have ever seen, especially when he stuck his hand under his pillow and retracted it with shit on his fingers, which he then rubbed on his face while trying to hold back the puke as he ran for the bathroom. Fat Phil and I both peed our pants. Of course, I received a beating for the turding and Fat Phil's involvement remained our secret.

The sister learned of our little plots and watched us closely for some time, until Fat Phil and I terrorized the kids that told on us and made it clear to all of them that all hell would come down on anyone that snitched on us to the sister. This worked for a while, and our plots went unpunished for the longest time. Eventually the sister got wise to us and set up a system of undercover snitches to report our every evil move. As a result of the undercover operation, Fat Phil's involvement was brought into the open and this resulted in his receiving a beating right along with me. Fat Phil always cried like a little girl, even though the sister barely touched him with the paddle. At first I thought that he could not stand pain like I could, but when his smile came through his tears as he walked past me on his way out of the beating room, it dawned on me that his brain had done it again. His crying act had succeeded in his getting a light whipping instead of a beating like mine. He told me that I should try it because it worked, but I told him that it was too late for me. The sister would know that I was faking it. I know that she would, for I had always thrown it in her face that the beatings would never bother me, never!

For a while the sister found out everything that we did, but Fat Phil's brilliant mind came through again. "We'll go undercover too," he said. From then on, we planned in secret, which took some of the fun out of it, because we liked to watch the looks on their faces when our heads touched in our plotting corner. Our outright laughing in their faces had to stop too. Most of the fun was gone and our little plots, although not as numerous, were harsher and more evil. They had become more of a tool to inflict pain upon those whom we didn't like and less and less just funny little evil pranks. I could sense a sincere feeling of dislike from the other kids, which was also new, because our pranks were no longer funny to everyone. Even with the fact that we never tried to molest anyone and often went so far as to stop other kids from being molested, it seems that even orphans, who have well-established behavior problems, have a disdain for meanness. Even the children from the dregs of society have a basic feel for what is right and wrong, and they have a sincere dislike for anyone who they feel is mistreating another, no matter who it is. If I learned anything during my time at Saint Joseph's, it is this fact. Everyone has feelings, and if you mistreat people or anyone that they care about, eventually you will pay for your actions. You will pay dearly, and I know this, for eventually it dawned on me that I had done wrong to everyone around me, and if I were on fire, no one, not one person, would piss on me to put it out.

The passage of time was never a concern to the kids in the orphanage, and it was only noticed when someone left to go out into the world. This was a hard lesson for me to learn. The one person I cared about in the whole world, my blood brother, Fat Phil, told me that his dad was coming to get him to take him home for good. I asked Phil why he wanted to go home if his father did such horrible things to him. "I know that my father loves me, and even if he does nasty things to me, he doesn't do it too often and it's not too bad," he said. I nodded in agreement as we walked to the big fence that surrounded the orphanage on all sides. The fence was covered with a fern that would close up when you ran your finger over it, and we liked to call it "touch me not."

"Maybe you should put some of this around that big old wiener of yours," I said. Phil looked at me for a moment and then smiled. Fat Phil touched one of the branches of the fern, and as it closed up at his touch, he told me how his father had made him put his penis into his mouth. He began to sob, and then came a painful deluge of tears as he went on and told me all the nasty things that his father had done to him and his sister. I had not known about his sister because she had died several years before I met Phil, and he had never talked about her. She was several years older than Phil, and she would sneak to Phil's room at night, and they would cry together after their father had finished with them. I begged Phil not to go home and to stay with me. We sat for the rest of the day on the grass, turning over rocks, looking for tarantulas, and talking until the whistle blew to come in for lunch. We sat and ate our peanut butter sandwiches and drank our Kool-Aid in silence, not looking at each other from across the room as we usually did. It was different now, and something was gone. After lunch I went to work in the kitchen, and Phil went to the playroom. I forgot to tell Fat Phil that we would see each other later to say good-bye, and I thought about how it would be when he was gone. As I walked down the dark hallway toward the kitchen, I suddenly wanted to go back and spend every remaining moment with Fat Phil. He was my friend, my blood brother.

All afternoon I kept thinking about Fat Phil as I washed the knives and pots and pans. Fat Phil was all that I had, everything that was good for me in the entire world. From the very first night, a night that was so terrible for me, when I was so afraid, afraid of everything and I didn't know what was going to happen to me, Fat Phil was there. He was there that first morning to tell me what to do after I had wet the bed and tried to hide it. He was a comfort to me always, the only comfort that I had in the whole world, and now he was going to leave. Suddenly, I became short of breath, and my heart began to pound out of control. He was really going to leave, and I would always be alone. I would have no one and nothing to live for.

I hadn't noticed that I had cut my finger. Silently, I looked at the blood dripping, and I was amazed at how little it hurt. I hadn't even known that I cut it. I began to think about Fat Phil and how he was my only true friend, the only person I could talk to. Phil was the only person I cared about, and now he was to leave the next day and I probably would never see him again. I thought about his father, an evil man, a man who would make Phil, his own loving son, suck his dick. I wished that I could kill Phil's dad, and then Phil would have to stay here with me. I fantasized about stabbing him with one of the big knives that lay before me on the counter. I would stab him in the heart and cut off his hands, and then I would cut off his penis and flush it down the toilet. Before I realized it, I had cut myself again, but like before I thought about how it hadn't hurt and how I hadn't even felt it when I had cut myself. I looked down at my shirt and noticed how dirty it was and then thought of how Sister Conchada would complain if she had to get me a clean one. I knew that I was in trouble already, and to top that off, Fat Phil was leaving in the morning. Something was suddenly wrong, and it took me several minutes of hard thinking to see what it was. I was all so clear for me now. I was alone. My father wanted to kill me and my mother had dumped me in this awful place that was supposed to be a holy place but was an evil place where evil things happen to small children. I could see it clearly for the first time. I saw things that I had denied even to myself, things like how the big kids molested the smaller kids and made them do unspeakable things. I had a vision in my head that I could not shake of my little brother, Mike, being molested by other boys with no faces, and I had nightmares of trying to chase them away but my feet would not move, even though I tried with all my might. I put my hands to my ears because I could now hear my brother calling me to help him, to make them stop.

Blood ran into my mouth from the cuts on my fingers, and I could taste it. I remembered that taste when my father had broken my jaw, and while I was thinking about the taste of blood, I ran the knife across my left wrist and saw a red line appear. Just as before, there was no pain, so without thinking I ran

34

the knife across my other wrist and a new red line appear. I stood there as the lines spread wide and watched the blood drip into the dishwater. I don't know how long I was standing there looking at the blood, but Fred approached with a load of pots and pans and noticed how red the counter and water were. He looked at me and saw what I had done. He screamed at me and started wrapping towels around my arms while dragging me to the office, where Sister Cooper sat reading a magazine with her feet up on the desk. She let out a squeal when she saw that I had cut my wrists. She roughly grabbed me and led me to the nearest sink, washed off my arms, and told me, "You stupid, stupid boy, what have you done?" I was the dragged down the long, dark halls and up the stairs to a room where I had never been before, with a sign on the door that said Medical. I remember looking around to see if this hallway was the way to get to the girls' side of the building, but no obvious clue was given. As we waited for the nurse, I watched the towels on my arms turn red. The nurse finally arrived, unlocked the door, and roughly washed my arms. She told me to stand near the sink so as not to make a mess. As I stood at the sink, I looked into the mirror at the scar across my chin. I stood there looking at it and opening and closing my mouth so that my injured jaw would make a clicking noise, which I knew would always annoy Sister Conchada, whom I knew would soon be summoned. As the nurse bandaged my arms, she told me that it looked worse than it really was, and that it was lucky that no stitches were needed because she didn't have any pain killers and it would have hurt very badly to sew the cuts without it. I just clicked my jaw.

As expected, Sister Conchada arrived in a huff, glaring at me as she listened to what the nurse had to say about me. She was told that I should sleep in the nurse's station tonight so that they could keep an eye on me. I knew that Sister Conchada was really angry at me but I also knew that she always had tomorrow for punishment and to get even. I was given a bed, which I was told to make up, and I sat on it until the nurse gave me a pill and a cup of water. Before leaving the room and turning out the light, she again called me a stupid, stupid boy. I peed the bed on purpose before I fell asleep.

The next morning Sister Conchada arrived just as I was getting my underwear out from under my pillow, where I kept them dry. I got dressed and put on my shoes as quickly as I possibly could. When I had finished, all she could say was "Come." At chapel I was placed in a special spot in the row behind the sisters. I wanted to look around to see if I could see Fat Phil, but I didn't because one was supposed to concentrate on prayers and it was not permitted to be looking around midprayer. I was placed at a table in a far corner by myself at breakfast, and I could not see if Fat Phil was there or not. I wanted desperately to see him one more time to tell him that I would miss him. Finally, from across the room, there he was, and my eyes met Phil's, and at that moment I knew that Fat Phil would always be my friend, my blood brother. I whispered to myself, and I imagined that Phil did the same: "Blood brothers forever." I was the first one led out of the dining hall, and I was taken directly upstairs to another hallway that I had never seen before and to a door that I didn't recognize. Silently, Sister Conchada opened the door and pointed inside with her crooked finger like there was something evil inside. "In" was all she said as she shoved me inside and slammed the door behind me. I was surrounded at first by total blackness, and then slowly the little room lightened up and I could see the light showing through from under the door. Standing in the dark for what seemed like hours and hours, my feet began to hurt, so I sat on the floor and leaned against the wall. There in the dark, I thought about Fat Phil, just little nothings at first, but then I realized that Phil was to leave today and go home to his father. I would not see him to say good-bye, and then I was suddenly on my feet and breathing very hard, and almost involuntarily I began to call for the sister. "Sister, Sister," I called over and over and louder and louder, but there was no response. Then I was pounding on the door and screaming at the top of my lungs, "Sister, Sister, please let me out, please." I knew that she could hear me because you could hear a pin drop in the long, dark hallways. After a while, I sat down and rested before trying again. "Sister, Sister, let me out!" I was hoping that Fat Phil would not leave without saying good-bye, and I knew that Phil was watching for me too. We were looking for each other, like good blood brothers should. I finally gave up on calling the sister because I knew that she would not come, so I sat on the floor and began to hum. It was not a particular tune I was humming, nothing that you would recognize, just a low combination of tones, almost a moan. I lay on the floor with one eye trying to look under the door, and humming. Hours later I was still lying on the floor in that dark closet, humming to myself, when the door suddenly sprang open and there before me were the black nursing shoes of Sister Conchada.

As she led me down the hall, I could tell by the smell in the air that it was lunchtime, and I dared not think that just maybe I could see Fat Phil one more time to say good-bye. I was happy, even though it wasn't apparent on the outside. I was happy on the inside. All the other kids watched as I was seated in the last chair at the last table in the dining hall. A peanut butter sandwich, some carrots, and a cup of Kool-Aid sat before me, but all that I wanted to do was find Fat Phil, and I was becoming desperate. I soon spilled the drink as I leaned over to see if Phil was there. I looked up and down each row of kids, and then I looked again, slower this time, but Phil was not there. He was gone and would never come back again, and it tore my heart out that I had not been able to say good-bye. Finally, I sat down and tried to eat the part of the sandwich that was not soaked when my drink spilled. I sat there in silence until I was told to go to the playground with the rest of the kids because I was not to go to work in the kitchen that day.

On the playground, a kid named Steven who sometimes would play cards with Phil and me, approached me and said, "Phil said to give these to you," and he handed me the old, worn-out deck of cards that Phil had cherished so much. He looked at the bandages on my arms as I reached for the cards, and then Steven left as quickly as he had come, as if he were afraid to stay near me. I looked down at the old cards with a rubber band that I had found and given to Fat Phil the day before. These were the cards that Phil always kept in his back pocket, his prize possession, and as I looked at them, I had to choke back the tears. I wanted desperately to cry, but I didn't. I never saw Fat Phil again, and I missed him terribly. If I had a picture of Fat Phil, this is where it would be.

After Fat Phil left, I decided that I didn't need any friends, and I therefore developed such an abusive manner that I made certain there was little chance of that occurring. I began to abuse the other kids verbally and physically, in all sorts of devilish ways. It was readily apparent to them that I wanted nothing more than to be left alone, and they gave me what I wanted. It wasn't long before I even stopped looking for Mike on the playground. Anyone that got in my way was either punched or kicked in the balls—anyone, no matter what shape or size. Come one, come all, I fought them. Anyone that got too close was punched, kicked, or hit by a rock. I wanted to be left alone.

I could sense that Sister Conchada was getting close to her wit's end, as she liked to say, because all of her mean, slicing comments suddenly turned to a cold, silent stare. I began to get beatings because she said I was constantly rubbing my penis. I didn't think to tell her that it itched, and once she noticed it, it seemed I was rubbing it all the time. She thought that I was unable to control this nasty habit, and as a result I received several severe beatings at the hands of Sister Conchada. Eventually she grew tired of my constant rubbing and called me into the tile room, where she brandished a butcher knife. Holding it up to my face, she said, "I'm tired of you constantly playing with yourself, and it has got to stop. If not, I guarantee you that I will cut it off. I could cut it off right now, and no one would say a thing, and no one would care. You are a nasty, stupid little boy, and no one cares what I do to you." Suddenly, I remembered what fear was, even though I had never really forgotten. I had just become a master at hiding it. I tried to get control of it and not to show my fear, but the sister could see that I was shaking in fear; she saw it in my eyes. She knew that I was afraid. She knew that she was back in control, and it wouldn't be long before I would jump when she spoke, and I did jump, at least for the rest of that day.

Late that night, I got up, got my underwear from under my pillow, and put them on along with the rest of my clothes. I crossed the big dormitory as quietly as I possibly could and then headed down the dark hallway. Down the stairs and out the big double-glass doors, out into the cool night air I crept. I paused for a while, there in the dark, and I was amazed at how bright the stars were, and I tried to remember if I had ever seen them at all, except through the windows in the playroom. They were so bright that I felt that I could almost touch them. I reached up for them and noticed that the bandage on my right arm was coming off, so I tore it off and walked to the big fence to touch the touch-me-nots. Against my will, Fat Phil crept into my mind, but I was unable to stop it. I pushed the memories out of my mind and up and over the fence I went. Landing solidly on the other side like, a cat, I grabbed and pulled the gate toward me and it swung open, enough for any man to go through the opening. I remember thinking how stupid I was, and I laughed to myself. Next time I'll try the gate first, I told myself. In the middle of the road, I looked left and then right. One way, I could see lots of lights and the other was totally dark. I decided to go toward the light.

As I walked, I began to think about what would happen when they found that I had run away. Certainly, no one would miss me. I imagined that all the kids would form a circle with Sister Conchada and go round and round, hand in hand, chanting, "Rocket dick is gone, Rocket Don is gone, yeah, yeah." I was in the city before I knew it, and I wandered around for several hours until I passed a coffee-and-doughnut shop. It smelled so good that I circled around to the rear of the building just to smell it. In the back I saw a man dump a tray of doughnuts into the garbage, and then he threw a cigarette on the ground and stepped on it before he went back inside. There, in that dark alley, I had myself a doughnut feast. I must have eaten ten jelly doughnuts, and they were so good that I put two more in my pockets before I continued down the street. I was waddling now because I was so full. I remember wishing that I had brought a coat with me because it was getting cold.

Without warning, I was almost blinded by a bright light, and from the light came a voice. "Where are you going, boy?" said the voice. At first I said nothing, thinking that I should run away, but when the question was repeated, I saw a big policeman walking toward me, coming out of the light.

Finally I said, "I'm going to the Sutter Candy Company."

The cop replied, "Where do you live, boy, and where are your mom and dad?"

"I ain't got no mom and dad." Upon that statement, he placed me into the backseat of the police car and down the road we went. I had been arrested.

On entering the police station, I was suddenly surrounded by police officers that were amused at what had been dragged into their midst. I was told to empty my pockets onto the table, which consisted of two mashed jelly doughnuts and an old deck of cards. I heard the cop that picked me up say, "Great." The dingy office had the heavy smell of cigarettes, and I remember trying to smoke a short butt that someone left smoldering in an old coffee can, but I threw it back when it made me cough. I was thirsty and asked for some water, but I was told that I would get nothing until I told them where I lived. The answer came right out before I could stop it. "St. Joseph's Orphanage," I told them, "but I don't want to go back."

"Why?" asked the cop.

I told them how Sister Conchada was going to cut off my wiener, but the cops laughed hysterically for several long minutes before they gave me any water. Upon further investigation, it was found that I had a rash on my penis, which itched and caused me to rub it all the time, and after a promise from the cops to protect me, I agreed to return to the orphanage. I enjoyed the ride in the police car, but it soon turned to fear again as the big, dark building came into sight. Sister Conchada was standing on the stairs as the car approached, having received a phone call from the police telling her that one of her kids had escaped and that they were to return him within the hour. I stood there in silence as the cop told her that I was wandering around town looking for some candy store. He also told her to have a doctor look at my penis because he thought that I might have some sort of infection, causing it to itch.

Inside, the nurse was awakened and summoned to the medical room to look at my wiener, and she was surprised to see the same little boy. I was told to drop my pants and underwear, which was normal around the sisters, and I expected to get a beating, but instead I was grabbed roughly and asked what was wrong down there. I said, "It itches."

"Skin it back," she said. I didn't know what she meant, so I just lifted it up and pulled it back.

"Further," she ordered, and I tried to pull harder, but I was tired and wanted to go to bed. At that point, the nurse grabbed my penis roughly and pulled the skin back so hard that it hurt, exposing a white substance and a rash below that was causing the itch. Some sort of medical salve was applied to my penis with a napkin, and she asked why I never cleaned it myself. I told her that I didn't know that I was supposed to. Impatient, the nurse wiped it roughly and said, "Like this, you stupid boy. Now you do it," she said. I was told to spend the rest of the night in the medical station bed, and the nurse checked the cuts on my arms before leaving and turning out the lights. The next day I was in the closet again, and it was there that I realized that I had left Phil's cards at the police station. I wanted to cry again, but I knew what to think of so I wouldn't, so I just sat on the floor and hummed and hummed, and I've been humming ever since.

My behavior got worse and worse, and the resulting punishments only made me meaner and tougher. The length of time that Sister Conchada and I spent together in the tile room seemed to get longer and longer. We would talk and talk for hours at a time, she sitting on the bench and me standing naked before her. She would talk about how she had grown up in Spain, living in total poverty. I told her that I thought that she was a Nazi because I had heard rumors about how she had worked in the death camps, none of which was true, she said. She had become a nun at the age of twenty-two. She told me that she had noticed that my penis would get erect when I received swats, and she asked why. I told her that I didn't know why, but our relationship grew more and more into a sexual experience than that of punishment. I asked her if she was going to cut off my wiener, and she promised me that she wouldn't.

One night in the beating room, she showed me a big rubber bottle with a hose that extended from it, and this, she said, would flush the evil right out of you. And with that, she bent me over and inserted the tube into my butt and squeezed the bottle. I could feel the warm water run down my legs, and I could see that it was turning brown and smelled of shit. "I've got to poop; I've got to poop" was all that I could say, and I just barely made it to the toilet before it gushed out. From then on, enemas were the rule of the day when it came to punishment with Sister Conchada, but my behavior did not improve.

On the second Christmas I spent at the orphanage, my mother came to visit, and it felt very strange at first because she was nothing like I had remembered. But I soon settled down into a pleasant visit. Mike had grown a couple of inches since I had last seen him, and I told him so. We all walked to the grotto to sit and talk. Mike wanted to know when my mother was going to take us away from this place and her reply was, "Soon." My mother had brought some crayons and a coloring book for Mike and a deck of cards for me. She also gave me a necklace with a cross on it, and she put it around my neck. She told me that the sisters had told her that I had a discipline problem and that I must be a good boy and obey the rules like she was sure that I would do for her. I promised that I would do better. The visit was over almost before it had started, or so it seemed. I was returned to the sisters, and then my mother was gone again. I was led away by the sisters. I wanted to cry, but I didn't.

I got into another fight the very next day, and I was so angry that I knocked the other boy's front teeth out. As a punishment, I was put back into the closet, but after what seemed like hours, I succeeded in getting the door open, and I made my escape. When I made my mad dash for the fence, it was just getting dark. This time I decided to go the other way, thinking that I would be far away by morning. It took some time, but I finally entered a gate and crept past two men who were talking and smoking cigarettes.

After passing several jeeps and trucks that were marked US Army, it dawned on me that I was on an army post. I was so excited, and I explored everything as I walked along. It was wonderful, and I knew that this is where I belonged. This is where I wanted to stay. I wanted to join the army, and I knew that I was tough enough to be a good soldier. I knew I could do it. As I explored, the lights started to come on, and other men were soon going about their way here and there, all in uniform. No one seemed to notice me wandering around, looking all raggedy and alone, until a soldier with an MP on his shoulder pulled up in a jeep and asked me, "Where do you think you're going?"

I said proudly, "I'm going to be a soldier."

This brought a loud laugh from the soldier, but I was still dragged down to a huge tent that had a sign saying, Officers' Mess.

Another soldier came over, looked down at me, and smiled. "So you want to be a soldier?" he said. I nodded. "If you're going to be a soldier, you'll have to act like one, and always tell the truth," he said, the smile disappearing. I nodded again. After asking me where I came from, I hesitated, but told him I was from St. Joseph's Orphanage. "We'll have to take you back, for a few years, but you come and see me when you're eighteen years old, OK?" he said. I nodded a third time, and I felt that big lump in my throat when I knew that I had to go back to St. Joseph's.

I became an instant celebrity when they took me through the chow line and let me choose my own food. I was told, "Take all you want, but eat all you take." I took more than I could eat, but no one said anything. A big black man came over and sat next to me and said that he had heard that I was an orphan. I told him that I had a mom but that she had left me there, and I didn't know if she was going to come and get me or not. He said that he was an orphan too, but now he had a family, and it was the US Army. He said that he had cooked all night and now he was going to take me back to St. Joseph's. His name was John, and he was from Virginia. He said he was proud to meet me as he shook my hand and smiled.

As John drove me back to the orphanage, I begged him not to take me back. I told them that the sisters were going to cut off my wiener when I got back. I begged and begged, but in the end, we arrived back just as breakfast was being served. I could see John looking at me as he drove off, and although I was led all the way there by my ear, I received a second breakfast.

After the bathroom period, I was pulled aside by Sister Conchada and told to strip my bed. I was told that I would be moving to a dorm where the older kids slept and that if I got into a fight there, all the kids would be bigger than me. Just as in my arrival in the other dorm, the bullies soon approached me, and they were ugly.

The result was that I got into several fights on the first day with the same kid. When the fights were broken up, I would stew and stew for a while, and then I'd sneak attack the kid until he finally got his fill of me and passed me on to the next bully. I received a beating from a new sister, which really got my attention with its ferocity. I thought that my ass was bleeding when she got done with me. "This behavior will not be put up with in this dorm," she said. That night, after lights out, I crept to the bully's bed and gave him as hard a whack in the mouth as I have ever hit anyone in my life. He was bloodied and screaming as he ran down the hall to squeal on me. As a result, I spent half the night standing with my nose to the wall before being told to go to bed. After that I was pretty much left alone by all the boys, which was fine with me. I found that my friend Fred, from the kitchen, was in my new dorm, and he had told the others to leave me alone. It seemed to work because no one bothered me too much after that. Fred and I would hang together because of our time together in the kitchen. I must have driven him crazy because he couldn't seem to escape me. I was everywhere.

The necklace with the cross that my mother gave me was the cause of my next fight. Quite by accident, a kid grabbed the necklace, breaking it. I was so mad that I kicked him in the balls and chased him as he ran to the sister. After being separated, it still wasn't over for me. I had an old fishhook that I had found, on a line that was about a foot long. I took this hook and swung it around, catching the kid square in the face, imbedding it deeply into his cheek. Bloodied and crying, he ran to the sister. After having to watch as she pushed the hook all the way through to cut off the barb, I was escorted to the priest's office. This I dreaded because I had heard all about the kids that were taken to the priest, and it wasn't a good thing. I was shaking in my shoes as I was told to stand on a certain square tile in the middle of the hall until I was called into his office. It wasn't long before the priest stormed out of the office directly to me, grabbed a handful of my hair, and dragged me into his office. I stood before this huge man, and he asked me if I thought I was a big man or something. I said, "No, but you sure are a big fat man." He slapped me across the face so hard that it knocked me over a chair, and I hit my head on the wall. When I got up, he slapped me again and beat me within an inch of my life before taking me to my closet, where I sat contentedly but hurt and hummed the time away.

After some time, the priest retrieved me and instructed me to clean the big bathroom floors with a toothbrush. It was there that I found that my neck hurt so badly that I could not turn my head and that there was blood running from my right ear. The bathrooms are so big that it took me most of the night to clean the floors with the toothbrush, so it was very late when I was finally led to the dormitory to go to bed. The next day, I could not walk, and when I tried to stand up, I got dizzy. I tried to stay in bed but was made to get up and go to chapel. There I threw up in front of everybody, and the entire chapel stank of vomit. One of the sisters whispered in my ear and told me to stay there when the other kids went to breakfast. After all the other kids had gone to breakfast, she gave me a bucket of hot, soapy water and some rags to clean up the vomit. Then she told me to stand with my nose to the wall for the remainder of the day. It was a long day, but I got through it because I did not get to eat, so I had nothing to throw up.

I wasn't told about it, but there was to be a special treat for all the kids that night. A movie would be shown that evening for the enjoyment of all. Fred whispered it to me as he passed on his way to work in the kitchen and said that everyone was so excited about it. The movie was about a robot called Robbie. I was very excited because I could not remember if I had ever seen a movie. I was taken to dinner, and afterward everyone was filed into the big room where Santa Claus would hand out presents at Christmas. Everyone sat on the floor in front of the big screen. I was about to sit on the floor next to my friend Fred when the priest grabbed me by the hair, led me to the front of the room, and instructed me to lie facedown, nose on the floor, with my arms spread out to my sides. He told me not to look up or I'd be punished severely. I could not see the movie, but I could hear it, so I enjoyed it that way, just like at my grand-father's when we would listen to the radio. I enjoyed it the only way I could. When the movie was over, he told me to lie there until everyone else had gone to bed, and then instructed me to clean the bathroom again before going to bed. My behavior improved after this incident, not because they had broken me but because they had something that I wanted: the movies. It was some-thing new to me, wanting something, and I did not know how to handle it.

Living in the big boys' dorm, I had a different time period on the play-ground. On the first day that it happened, I almost missed him. I walked right past him and he right past me. It struck me as funny that I didn't even know my own brother, but that was the truth of the matter. I turned and asked if he was Mike, and he asked if I was Keith. No hugs, no kisses, no affection at all, and that was that; we walked our separate ways. It took several meetings like this before we warmed up to each other, and even then it was not like I imagined it should be between brothers. We were brothers, and it was a dirty shame that I didn't have more time to get to know him the way I should have, but it was the way it was there in the orphanage. Affection of any kind was seen as a weakness of sorts. I felt that if I loved my brother, in time it would be torn from me and I would suffer. I didn't dare ask if he had been molested, for I knew that he must have because he was so small and could not defend himself, so I just didn't ask, and he never mentioned it either. In the past, I had suffered greatly because of affection, and in the past I had beaten it. I was reluctant to let it back in, but I did so anyway, to a certain degree, because I couldn't help it.

Mike looked so small and sad that I became very angry and went into his dorm and walked down the isles between the beds and hit every kid I got close enough to as hard in the face as I could. I made sure that everyone knew that I was Mike's brother and that I would be back if anyone touched him again. I didn't see it coming, but I was hit so hard from behind that it knocked me unconscious and left me lying on the floor until I looked up to see a big fat nun looking down at me. After that, and a short beating, and I was back in my closet. I didn't show much affection for Mike, but I loved him, and I know that Mike felt the same way because I could sense that he was holding back, and I did not hold it against him because I understood his reasoning. Maybe someday it would change, but not today, and I was sure that it wouldn't be tomorrow either. Our meetings would always be casual and friendly, and I treated him as I would have treated Fat Phil.

I truly tried to be good, but it always seemed as if I was the target of the older kids. Slowly and surely I began to fit in. Soon they were teaching me the big-boy games like poker, rummy, and football and baseball. The more I seemed to fit in, the better my behavior became. I learned how to lie, cuss, cheat, and how to give someone the finger, which got me into no end of trouble. My schedule was as follows:

6:30 a.m. Chapel
7:30 a.m. Breakfast
8:00 a.m. School
Noon. Lunch
2:30 p.m. Work in the kitchen
6:00 p.m. Play room
7:00 p.m. Chapel
8:00 p.m. Bathroom time
8:15 p.m. Bedtime

I really didn't mind things as they were because it made the time pass quickly, and I knew that when I was old enough, I would run away and they would never catch me. I did not do well in school, and I was placed with kids that were much younger than I was, so of course there were those who took advantage of that fact. All sorts of new nicknames arose out of the fact that I was so dumb. I felt dumb too.

Of course the usual fights arose out of it also. My little meetings with Sister Conchada continued on a regular basis, and soon I began to enjoy them. I began to enjoy the things that she did to me, and I enjoyed the way that she touched me. As you can imagine, soon I was getting in trouble just to see her. I would strip naked almost before I got in the door, and I was always excited at her touch. Sometimes she would bathe me after the enema, and this, above all, was what I enjoyed. She became as close to me as my mother had ever been. I was in love with her, and I hated her at the same time. These sessions would continue, almost until the day I left the orphanage.

While working in the kitchen, I sometimes could see across to the girls' side, and this was the point of much discussion among the boys. One girl in particular was the center of my attention. She was about my age and had black, raving hair. I could see the beginnings of small breast swelling beneath her blouse, and this brought out all sorts of new feelings within me. Soon I was fantasizing that we were boyfriend and girlfriend, and I invented a name for her, Sara. We were always exchanging glances. At least in my mind, we were passing love at each glance, and I was in love with her for years. I never talked to her, I never knew her name, but I loved her, and I know in my heart that she loved me too. I think that I was caught several times practicing kissing my arm in case I ever got the chance for a real kiss from my imaginary lover. At one meal, candy was passed out to each child. They were large chocolate drops with a white creamy filling, and they were so good. Working in the kitchen, any extra candy was divided among the child workers, and it was then that I got a glimpse of the box that it came in. Right on the side, in big red letters, was the name Sutter Candy Company. I was so excited to see it that I almost choked on my candy. I imagined that Fat Phil had sent it just for me, and everyone else got lucky, but I know that it was from him, not his pervert father. I again had hopes of seeing Fat Phil again, but it soon passed, and it was not to be.

Time went steadily by. From time to time, I would see Mike on the playground, going in as I was coming out. Occasionally I would have a nightmare about some crazy old man trying to kill me, and then I would wet the bed, get spanked, and get made fun of by the other older kids, and this was my life for the remainder of my stay at St. Joseph's Orphanage. Five times a month, I would line up, strip off my old clothes, throw them in a pile, and await my turn to be fitted with clean clothes. I must have been a sight, standing there in pants that were too short, a shirt that was too little, and holes in my underwear and socks, always. This was all there was.

This was my life, and it rarely changed, but I was surprised with a visit from the soldier that had taken me to the chow hall the day that I had run away. He had remembered my name and had asked for me. He wanted to take me out for the day to a carnival that was down the road, between the orphanage and the army post. At first I didn't trust him, but I spent the entire day with him, riding the rides, and eating candy, cotton candy, and hot dog. I'm not sure if he even knew that I enjoyed myself because I was quite shy and quiet, but I did have a good time. I don't know if I told him that or not, but I distinctly remember thanking him when he returned me to the orphanage that evening. He had given me a little round aluminum medal with my name engraved on it, which I soon lost in the laundry, to be eaten by some machine. I never forgot his name—John—and I've always been thankful for him. I have remembered that day as one of the few good days that I had during my stay at St. Joseph's. I had hoped to see him again, but it was not to be, and I never saw him again. Some of the kids asked me what I was doing with "that nigger" all day, and as you can guess, the fights were on.

Like I said before, the passing of time was never noticed unless some important event occurred that became a mark in time that we would use as sort of a calendar, something to judge the amount of time that had passed since the last big occurrence. As I got older, I noticed more and more of what was happening around me. There were always the bullies, but now there seemed to be more and more of the bullies that would do nasty things to the smaller kids. I think that it was always going on, but I never seemed to notice it except on my first night in the orphanage when two bullies were looking at my brother's penis, and I had gotten a punch in the face when I stopped them. All this time, it was as if I had a blind eye to it as long as they left me alone. Now I found myself fighting more and more for the protection of some little guy that couldn't fight for himself. After it happened once, it seemed to happen more and more. It's as if word got around that I was the one to come to if you needed help. I always seemed to put my nose where it didn't belong, but I could not stand to know what was going on and then to do nothing about it. I just couldn't. As a result, the closet seemed to be my second home, for that was the only punishment that they knew that I could not stand. In the closet I would try to remember my mother and what she looked like, but I couldn't remember her face. I couldn't remember what Tony looked like either. At times I was left in the closet so long that I had to use the bathroom, usually in my pants, and that always angered the sisters.

More and more kids would come to me crying and telling me all the horrible stories about how this person or that had made him do this or that, and they would plead for me to help them. Sometimes I could, and sometimes I couldn't. I can remember trying to help a kid named Gerald Elmore. Gerald had come to the orphanage about a year prior, and he had told me that his father had owned a worm ranch and fishing bait store, but he and his father both had gotten sick. He had recovered, but his father died. Gerald was a sickly looking kid with a mouthful of rotten teeth. He was taller than I was, but he was much thinner and always seemed to be sick or look sick. Two brothers named Slater were picking on Gerald. At one time I had hung around with one of the Slaters, the younger one named Gary. For some reason the Slater brothers had taken a disliking to Gerald, and they always seemed to be hitting him or pushing him down.

Gerald ran to me on the playground, yelling my name and spitting blood all over me when he hid behind me as the Slater brothers chased him. I tried to walk away and pull Gerald along to get away, but the older Slater wouldn't have it. In an instant, he and I were toe-to-toe and slugging it out. He was bigger and older than I was, and I was on the losing side of the fight when his brother jumped in and tried to hold my arms while his brother thumped on me, but I got a good one in on the younger Slater's nose, and he ran away crying. At that, the older boy backed off, and from that day on, Gerald was always at my side, and he never seemed to shut up. Gerald was like my shadow for a long time, and for some reason he kept me out of trouble. I think it was the way he thought about things in such an open and honest way that rubbed off on me and kept me on the straight and narrow. Anyway, it kept me from being locked in the closet so much, and Sister Conchada brought that fact to my attention during one of our little sessions in the beating room.

The little sessions with Sister Conchada always went the same way, in that she would always be angry at first and yell at me to strip naked. She would beat me with the wooden paddle. Almost instantly, she would give me an enema, with a hateful look on her face, until the water turned dark and stinky and I would have to go to the toilet. Then her mood would change, and she would act almost motherly. She would wash me in the shower or a tub and stroke me in a way that made me look forward to going to the beating room more and more. Sometimes she would make me stand before her naked and wet while she questioned me about my whole day. She always knew when I was lying as if she were watching me all day to see what I was doing. I don't know how she could have because I would look for her, and it was a rare occasion when I would spot her at all. The fact that I was no longer assigned to her dormitory didn't seem to affect the number of times I would receive punishment from her, but Sister Cooper, who ran the dormitory for the older boys, was much more brutal with her punishment, but they were few and far between and she demanded and received respect from all the boys simply because of the ferocity of the beatings that she would administer. Even I was afraid of her, and that was something because everyone knew that I was afraid of nothing. To tell the truth, when Sister Cooper was around, I was a very good boy all the time.

It wasn't too many months later that I was pulled out of the kitchen and taken to the laundry room without explanation. There I was fitted with probably the best clothes that I had ever been given during my time at St. Joseph's. It was only after I was dressed that I was told that my mother was coming to get me. I had no idea if I would be back or not, so the whole idea was foreign to me. I was told to gather up all my belongings while I stripped my bed and turned in the dirty bedding. The only things that belonged to me were a broken necklace, a deck of cards that I had received one Christmas, and a few pictures that I had torn from a magazine. I was led down a dark hallway and through a big double doorway, and there stood my mother, with Mike at her side. It was all so strange to me, and even though I had often dreamt of leaving, I really never thought I would. I looked at Mike and wondered at how big he was, and I couldn't help thinking about whether some sister had stuck things up his butt and touched him on the wiener. At this thought, I glanced around for Sister Conchada, and there she was, standing in the shadows. I couldn't see her face, but I sensed that she was sad to see me go, for I knew that she loved me. She had told me so, many times. I looked away for a second, and when I looked back, she was gone. I would never see her again, and I did not miss her. My attention turned back to Mike, and I wondered if the other boys had done things to him, bad things that I had seen some boys doing to others in my own dorm. Things that I knew nothing about but knew they were not natural, not right. I pushed it from my mind, and I grabbed Mike's hand, for I could tell that he was afraid, and after all, I was his big brother, wasn't I? I did not look around or say good-bye as we walked out the door. I just wanted to forget about the orphanage, and I said a prayer that I would never have to go back again. And I never did.

Three

Mike and I were alone in a strange car with another strange man, who sat next to my mother in the front seat. I can remember my mother trying to make polite conversation for a brief period as we drove down the strange road. I'm sure that she was trying to break the ice, but it didn't seem to be working, and soon we were riding in complete silence. I looked at the back of my mother's head and wondered why she had put us in that place. I could not know what she had gone through any more than she could know about what had happened to me. All that I knew was that I was very angry with her, and I wondered if we could ever love each other like we should. It dawned on me that I barely knew her and didn't know what she had planned for us in the future. I remember asking her where we were going to go now, and her reply made me feel somewhat better about what was going to happen to me. We were to live in a three-bedroom apartment in a housing development for people who didn't have very much money. She said that the only way she could afford the apartment was because the government paid most of the rent and gave us most of the food that we would eat. She tried to explain that it wouldn't be easy, but we would be together as a family. She said that my older brother, Tony, was waiting for us and that we now had another brother and sister, Dennis and Diane, that were twin babies.

I knew that I would have to take things as they came, and I decided that it had to be better than the orphanage, but I was still angry and would stay angry for a long, long time. My relationship with my mother and Tony would always be strained and distant, even though I did learn to love them again. The housing project located in South Little Rock was just about as poor a neighborhood as you would ever want to see. The kids on the street looked as if they were straight out of an orphanage, so I knew that I would fit right in, and I did. This project was where I would meet my first real girlfriend, and it was on the first day of school that I first met her. I'll never forget her name because I thought it seemed to sing when you spoke it. Her name was Cathy Molly, and she lived on the next block.

At the end of the first day of school, several black kids approached me and asked if they could feel my hair because it looked so fine. I said that they could if I could feel theirs, and that was the first time that I touched Cathy. The encounter was short, and they all left me standing on the corner watching them leave. I thought nothing of it, and went on home, where Tony was in charge while my mother was at work. I had seen Tony's type many times in the orphanage, and I knew right away that he was a bully. Force was his way, and he was good at it, for he soon had Mike and I doing his bidding whenever he wanted. He had a heavy hand and was quick to use it. Mike and I stayed clear of him as much as we could, but we were instructed to take care of Dennis and Diane, and we did most of the housework while Tony did most of the order giving. Tony's word was the rule, and there was no debating with him about anything. He was used to getting his way, and he was not about to change just because Mike and I had come to live there. Tony was the boss, and that was that.

The next day at school, I received a note that said, "I like you, do you like me? If you do, check yes or no in the box below." I checked the yes box because it was signed by Cathy Molly. From that moment on, we were inseparable, and soon I was spending every free moment I had with her. We always played at her house because Tony always seemed to have chores for me if I went home. It wasn't too long before we were kissing on the swing set and walking hand in hand everywhere we went. Cathy Molly was wonderful, and I felt that I was in love with her forever. Cathy's mother didn't seem to mind that I was a white kid, and the subject never arose with her. Sometimes when we walked together, we could hear comments from other people, but it didn't seem to matter to us at all, and for about six months we were together always. This came to an abrupt end when her father came home to find us kissing on the swings. He was all in a huff when he grabbed me and told me to get away from his daughter. He was a huge black man, with hands that could crush the life out of me if they wanted, but he succeeded in scaring the hell out of me. I remember his exact words. He said, "Get away from my daughter, and stay away. Don't ever come around her again, ever." After that Cathy wanted nothing to do with me, or so it seemed, but every once in a while I would find little things on my front porch that I knew belonged to her, necklaces or barrettes or some little notes that I knew were hers. I knew that she still loved me but that she was afraid to be around me. That was the end of Cathy Molly for me, but I will always have her in my heart. I will always remember her little secret gifts, given in the only way that she knew how, given to the little white boy who would always be her first love.

Upon leaving the orphanage, the first thing I had done in the little bedroom that Mike and I shared with Dennis and Diane was set up a little altar, a sort of shrine to God. It consisted of a picture of Christ, my little cross off of my broken necklace, and a piece of woven palm branch. Mike and I held our own little chapel daily at our little altar, much to the amusement of my brother Tony. This went on for months because our main prayer was never to have to return to the orphanage. I guess that my prayers were answered because within a month or two, we all were moved to Peoria, Illinois, to live with my uncle Carlee. Uncle Carlee had purchased an apartment building and offered my mother an apartment at a cheap rate if she would clean and cook for him. My mother jumped at the chance to get out of Arkansas, which she had come to hate.

At first, I didn't care much for my uncle because I found him to be fat and, I thought, lazy. He would sit on the porch and watch me do the yard work and help my mother clean house. It took some time, but I slowly grew quite fond of him, and I began to spend a lot of time with him. Sometimes I would go to work with him, and we would eat bologna sandwiches and look at books with naked girls in them. He was nuts about women of any type and always had the time to watch as they passed by. This seems to have rubbed off on me because I still catch myself sneaking peeks at passing women. Eventually I got a paper route, and I didn't have much time to hang out with my uncle, but we were always friends. He was closer to me than my own two brothers.

While folding papers one day, I read an article about a lady that had been sent to jail for keeping her kids locked away in a closet. Apparently, a neighbor had turned her in for being cruel to her kids, and I couldn't help but think about whether or not they had picked up the habit of humming some elusive tune that they were unable to break. Try as I may, I am still unable to stop humming whatever tune it is that I hum, and I guess I never will.

Just before I entered the eighth grade, two years late, my mother got a job at the post office, which enabled her to buy her own house. She met a man and eventually married him, and so he became my stepfather. He would be the only father that I would ever have. I grew to love him very much, and I have many fond memories of the time that I spent with and around him. He had found his first wife lying dead on their bedroom floor, and he had been alone for many years until he found my mother. He had three grown children of his own, and I know that it was not easy to take on five new ones. He was quite a man, and I loved him. I was not there when he died. I did not go to his funeral. At the end of his life, I probably only talked with him a few times a year. All this considered, it's probably hard to understand me when I say that I know that he knew that I loved him then, and I still love him, even now that he is gone. He was a kind and gentle man, and he taught me how to be kind and gentle. He taught me how to be a man. His name was Charles Hanley.

After they married, they bought a house in East Peoria. Tony would go away to the army, and I would attend high school, and it would be the happiest time of my life. I began to make friends easily, and soon I fit like a glove in our tiny little community. I was always older than my classmates, so I enjoyed what I call taking the lead. I was not the smartest, but I was always the toughest and fastest. I can safely say that my entire eighth grade was fight-free, and that was a real accomplishment for me. During the summer just before my freshman year in high school, I met and fell instantly in love with a girl named Penny Paluska.

This girl and I would spend almost all of our free time together for the next five years. Her father, Louie, was a plumbing contractor, and he and his wife, Betty, owned a little house with a pool near my house. I grew up in their house and became as close to a son to them as anyone ever will. I have the fondest memories of growing up with Penny in their little house. I was already sixteen years old when I began my freshman year, so I already had a car. Penny and I rode to school together almost every day. We always left a little early so as to have a little make-out time. I would pick her up every morning and drop her off every night, go home and eat dinner, and then was back at Penny's house until it was time for me to go home for bed. I was part of the Paluska family for years and years. When they asked me about my age, I told them about the orphanage, and it was never mentioned again. I was happy there, and for the first time in my life, I was happy about everything. I was truly in love with Penny, and we fully expected to spend the rest of our lives together, talking often about getting married after high school.

My freshman year could not have been any better. It was almost perfect. I tried out for and made the football team, as a fullback. I was going with one of the cutest girls in the whole school, a cheerleader, and I was a fullback on the freshman football team. These two combined placed me squarely in the middle of the in crowd. Oh yes, I was cool! Everybody knew that I was cool. I could dance with the best of them, even though I had no idea what I was doing on a dance floor. I guess that I looked cool, so that's all that mattered. Everyone was my friend, even the ones that no one else would talk to. The poor dressers and the not so cute were my friends, and I always took time to be with them if I could. I became the protector of the oppressed and soon garnered a reputation as a boy who would fight anyone, anywhere, at the drop of a hat.

The most important event of my freshman year occurred when I happened to see a boy who I recognized as a senior flirting with Penny in the stands as she watched one of my football games, after which I charged up the rows of seats, still in my uniform, and challenged him to a fight after school. He accepted, and we were to meet up on the hill after school the next day. At school the following day, I was of course the center of attention because I was a freshman who was going to fight a senior. Everyone fully expected me to get my ass kicked, but I knew better. I knew what damage I could do. After school, we met and walked up the hill together, talking as went along. The boy I was to fight was named Mike Couth, and he was also in the in crowd and on the varsity football team. A large crowd awaited our arrival were ready for the fight when we arrived at the area, designated as the school battlefield. Mike seemed to want to talk for a while, but I was ready and wanted nothing of chitchat. We were in the center of a large crowd, seniors and his friends nearest, and the freshmen, my friends, on the outside of the circle. Mike Couth had no idea how much I loved to fight, and I wanted to make an example of him to ward off anyone thinking of getting close to my Penny.

While he was still trying to chitchat, I was on him before anyone expected anything. He found himself on his back, bleeding all over himself, before he knew what had happened. I was on top of him, smashing his face with a hundred punches that he could not even attempt to block. It was so easy for me that I even let him up and told him that I was sorry I had started without him. I even helped him brush himself off before asking if he was ready to start again. As soon as he nodded, he found himself on his back again, trying to block my punches. It was pitiful, and I finally decided to take it easy on him when I found myself being dragged off of him roughly. I was fully prepared to fight the new person, until I came face-to-face with my football coach. "Get to practice, Sanders," he said. While turning to face the senior, he retorted, "You've got to watch out for these freshmen, Couth." This brought laughter from the crowd and the fight ended.

The next day at school, I was BMOC. From that day forward, no one, I mean, no one would mess with Penny Paluska, and I'm sure that it bugged her to no end because everyone knows how much high-school girls like to flirt. Penny was my girl. There was no mistake about it either. We would be together all the way through the four years of high school, including the summers in between. Penny was a lifeguard at the public pool, and I just hung around, lazing in the sun. It was perfect. It was just the way that I'm sure that some kids could only dream about, and I was living it. I was a popular football player and she was a popular cheerleader and we were perfect together. We were the perfect couple, and everyone knew it. When it came time to elect the prom king and queen, no other couple was even considered, and when it was announced that Penny and I were king and queen of the junior prom, no one was surprised. I really mean it when I say that it was a perfect time for me;

it really was. I played on the varsity football team as a second-string fullback behind one of the best players in the state of Illinois, and as a result, I only got to play in one game for two lousy plays. Just by luck, a photographer from the local newspaper captured those two plays on film and published them in the paper for all to see. What a spot of luck, because it made me look all the better. I tell you, everything was going my way, it really was, and it continued through my senior year through the following summer, which was our last summer together.

Penny went away to college at Western Illinois University, and I went to work at the TPW Railroad as a yard clerk. It was the fall of 1968 when it all fell apart for me, and I would never be able to get it back, ever. The Vietnam War was raging in the east, and the blacks were raging in the west, and I was in the middle. The whole world was about to come crashing down on me, and all I could think about was getting married to Penny. It was all consuming, and when I watched the children of our fathers dying every night on the TV news, it didn't concern me at all; I was somewhere else, not there. I had thought about joining the army, but that was in the far-off future, not now. I was too busy being happy and planning for the future. Oh, I was too cool to go to the army just now, or so I thought. It was all coming down for me, and I didn't even see it coming. I knew that my mother was concerned, but we hadn't talked much about it. Like the plague, the draft kept coming to the forefront of our conversations. It wasn't too much later that I received a letter stating that I was considered as A-1, prime draft material. With this first step, my world began to fall apart.

I began to notice a change in me when I realized that sooner or later I would be in the military and would probably have to go to war. I could feel it come over me, just as it had the day that my mother left me at the orphanage. It was the same feeling, the same emotions. My world was crashing down around me. I began to pay new heed to the newsreels shown daily of the raging war in Vietnam. There were boys dying in the mud every day, and it was shown on TV. It was real entertainment, to be enjoyed by all while they ate their dinner and watched the mayhem on the news. Boy, how they made it so glamorous. It almost made you want to go to war. Yes, I think that was probably why they put it on TV, so some kid would see it and want to be there, like gladiators in the arena of Rome, on TV for all to see. Scores were kept and published daily of exactly how many American kids had been killed by the Communists and exactly how many enemy kids had been killed by the Americans. It was wonderful. What a great job they did, filling me and millions of other American boys with *crap!* That's exactly what it was, but they called it propaganda. What a fancy name for crap! I was drawn to the TV every day; I couldn't take my eyes off it. They were killing my American brothers, and it was entirely their fault. They had to be stopped; they had to be stopped now, and I had to help. I had to do my part.

Slowly, I began to realize what was always expected of me, me and every other boy my age throughout the entire world. We were all destined to face each other on the battlefield. No one knew why, exactly, but from the very moment that I was born and brought into this world, it was my destiny. From my earliest memory, I had been always been aware of the soldiers of the world, and I knew from the beginning that sooner or later my time would come, and my time was here and now. It was circling me like a dark cloud of misery and despair. I could sense it coming, and when I realized that fact, I began to surrender to it. I was a fool, and so were millions of other boys just like me, all over the world. We all surrendered to it, and we would all suffer greatly for it. Of course none of us knew it then. I wish we had, but we didn't.

Mike was the first to go because he had quit high school and joined the US Marine Corps and was home on leave with orders for Vietnam when I decided to do my duty and join the army. I can remember vividly our conversation when I asked him what the service was like. "It's no game," he said. And that stuck with me for years afterward. It was no game! Suddenly I found myself in the recruiter's office and signing the papers for enlistment. I found myself wanting to go as soon as I could; I wanted to be a soldier like my father and his father before him. I would have to go sooner or later, anyway, because the draft board was taking everybody except married medical students. I knew it would be just a matter of time. This was my reasoning, my big, bright idea. I knew everything. I was brilliant, and this was a brilliant idea. Yes, I'll join the army. And I did.

I was given a train ticket to the reception station in Chicago and a pass to stay overnight at the YMCA that was located within walking distance of the reception center, and within two days I found myself sitting on the train, bumping along, with a shit-eating grin on my goofy face. Boy, I had the world by the balls. I knew everything; I knew exactly how it would be, from start to finish. I would be very brave, go to war, commit some heroic act, get lots of medals, be a hero, and then come home and marry Penny. From there it was all downhill, you know, happy ever after and all that crap. That was how it would be, and I was sure of it, as sure of it as I was that the United States would win the war. I was going to be like Horiatis Cocles, a soldier in the Roman army of 508 BC who single-handedly held off the entire Etruscan army on the Sublician Bridge. The Etruscans were so impressed with this one soldier that they ended their siege of Rome and returned home. As a reward for his heroic actions, a statue was erected in his honor and he was given all the land that he could plow around in one day. Yeah, I was exactly like old Horiatis; I was sure of that.

Four

arrived at the reception center right on time and was instructed by a big fat sergeant to get into a long line that I could not see the end of. It took about an hour before I was interviewed by another sergeant who I told that I wanted to be in the Green Berets. He politely wrote everything down and then instructed me to get into another line, which I did. After another hour or so, I was told to strip down to my underwear and then get into another line, which I did. For the next couple of hours, I was poked and prodded in every part of my body, and sometimes twice. I found out that I was color blind when I couldn't pass the color test but was relieved when they asked me to tell them which of two balls was red and which was green. After correctly answering, I was told that I had passed the entire test and that I would be accepted into the great, grand, US Army. Upon getting dressed, we were all sworn into the service of the United States Army. I was then instructed to return to the very first desk to be reinterviewed. There I was informed that my colorblindness would keep me from qualifying for the Green Berets, so after some quick thinking, I blurted out that I wanted to be a clerk. It was probably the smartest thing that I had ever said. The fat sergeant said, "OK," and that was that. My destiny was fulfilled. I was a soldier.

I returned home to say good-bye to all, and Penny informed me that she had joined a peace movement and would be protesting the war on all fronts. It was the first time that we had split on anything, the first of many to come. I was hoping to have sex with Penny before I left, but it was not to be. We had never really gone all the way before, even though I had told all my friends that we had, on a daily basis. Don't get me wrong, I knew every inch and curve of

61

Penny's beautiful body, every smell, every taste, and I loved it and wanted it even more, but it was never to be, for I was off the next day, bound for basic training at Fort Leonard Wood, Missouri.

The first thing that struck me was the sergeant's change in attitude when he spoke to us; he wasn't nice anymore. As a matter of fact, he was downright nasty, so I stopped asking stupid questions and sat quietly on the bus as we headed for Fort Leonard Wood. I found, through conversing with fellow passengers, that the post had a nickname of Little Korea because it was so hot in the summer and cold in the winter. I was also told that this particular time of year was the worst time to take basic training because it would be miserably cold, and boy, was that guy right. I remember thinking of how I'd have to toughen up if I was going to survive, and that's when I first encountered the biggest, toughest, meanest, blackest son of a bitch I had ever met. He appeared out of nowhere as soon as the bus stopped. "My name is Sergeant Dearing, and I am your worst nightmare" were the first words out of his mouth. He had a way about him that demanded attention, or it could have been his big German shepherd that was growling and trying to bite the man nearest him. "From now on, you will do what I say, when I say it," he screamed at the top of his lungs. "Do you understand?" His screaming drew a few answers that were more like mumbles than words. This response seemed to infuriate him, and he seemed to scream all the louder. "Get your asses off this fuckin' bus, now," he said loudly. It was all very threatening how they lined us up next to the bus and took turns screaming in our faces. After several gruesome minutes of this, we were lined up and pushed into a mess hall just like the one I had eaten at as a kid and were given five minutes to eat before being herded right back out again. We were then run down the street and forced into a building they called the barracks and told to get a good night's sleep because "the shit was on tomorrow," as he put it.

Before I could pick out a bunk, a fight erupted between a goofy-looking white guy and a huge black man who could have passed as a heavyweight boxer. It was over as soon as it began, and then the black guy started to look around for another sucker. When he looked at me, I just held up my hands and said, "I'm just looking for a bunk," so he just walked right past me and socked another guy. I found that this behavior was a good way to get thrown out of the army, or so I was told. I got as much sleep as I could, but with all the crying and moaning and complaining, it wasn't much. It helped a lot when they finally turned the lights out.

Sgt. Dearing appeared out of the darkness, blowing a whistle and screaming at what I thought was the top of his lungs, but I was definitely wrong about it being the top. He had unbelievable range when it came to his vocalization of his orders. Like a dumb shit, I said, "Good morning, Sergeant."

He said, "Shut your facehole, you asshole. If I want any shit outta you, I'll scrape it off your teeth. *Do you understand me!*"

I replied, "Yes, Sergeant."

"Yes, Drill Sergeant, you fuckin' asshole bastard. Where the fuck are you from, Asshole Land?" With this, he threw me bodily into the aisle and told me to give him fifty pushups, his big nasty looking dog chewing on my leg the whole time. I was extremely glad when he moved on to the next poor bastard and started yelling at him. We received about an hour of abuse at his hands before being given five more minutes for breakfast, and we were pushed out as fast as we were pushed in.

At a running pace we were herded down the street, and pushed into a building that said Supply on the door. We were told, in between scolding and pushups, that we were to be issued clothing and boots, and they were to be placed inside the duffel bag that we would be given. Anyone that did not follow orders immediately would proceed to get his ass kicked in a most proficient manner, and then he asked if we understood, and then asked again when he didn't like the response. We soon learned the proper response and were quick in giving it. Slowly the line began to move until I was given a duffel bag and a whole shitload of other things that I was supposed to fit into said duffel bag. Of course it all wouldn't fit, so I was trying my best to carry the whole armload of clothing without dropping any. This, I soon found, was impossible, and soon everybody was tripping over everybody else's stuff that had fallen all over the floor. I would fall, drop my stuff, and pick it up, over and over, until I thought I finally had it under control. It was at that moment that another duffel bag was thrown into my face, and I was told to place my web gear into that one while I fought to keep from dropping the other one. The speed at which the line was moving through the building increased at every turn, and at every turn there was a drill instructor screaming at you to get your shit together. Helmet, web belt, vest, and all other assorted gear were thrown directly into your face at every turn, and dropping something drew a barrage of insults from every direction. Finally, I could see the exit door in the distance, and I could hardly wait to reach it, thinking that I would be given time to get my shit together, as they say.

When I finally reached the door, I passed through into the open air and found that I was on a loading dock about four feet above the ground. Of course I dropped about half of my gear when I passed through the door. Waiting for me there stood the devil man, Sgt. Dearing. He reached over and grabbed me by my shirt, swung me in a circle, and then threw me off the dock to the ground below, where I landed with a thud. Almost before I hit the ground, the German shepherd was on me, chewing on my leg again and keeping me from standing up, so that I couldn't pick up my gear. I was called every name in the book, face-to-face with Sgt. Dearing, at a distance of three inches. This went on for what seemed like hours, and then it got worse. Forced to run a long distance, trying to hold onto my gear while receiving the insults and abuse of Sgt. Dearing, I pushed my way through the crowd of men who were falling and dropping their gear all over and finally arrived at a spot where we were told to line up and stand at attention.

After counting off, we were taken into the building and given a lecture about how our gear was to be stored, and then we were given half an hour to perform this impossible task, and with this new failure we were subjected to many, many more hours of unspeakable evils, which would continue for several weeks. That first day was the worst day for me in my training, and from that time on, it became easier and easier for me. I considered myself to be in pretty good shape, but within weeks, I felt that I was in the best condition of my life. Some of those poor devils had problems keeping up, and as a result there was no end to their suffering. I began to feel good about the training and knew the good that it was doing me. I felt myself changing from a boy to a man, and it felt good. We were being transformed into soldiers whether we liked it or not, and slowly but surely, we became a fighting unit. We became as one. We were becoming soldiers. When rifles were handed out, there was no mistaking the fact that we were coming around. It had taken a lot of hard work, and it was finally paying off. Soon we were marching as well as any platoon on the post. I felt good, and I was becoming confident that I could do any duty that I was assigned, and I did.

Sgt. Dearing had invested many hours of work into our training, and he was good at his job, for in the end we were STRAC troops. I had learned early never to volunteer for anything because the one time that I had was a disaster. At formation, Sgt. Dearing called for volunteers that could type. Thinking that I would get an easy day out of it, I raised my hand, as did several others. At that point we were told that everyone that raised his hand was to report for KP in the kitchen. This wasn't too bad because I was raised in the kitchen at the orphanage and felt comfortable there. Anyway, the point was never to volunteer for anything, for it always led to no good. After this moment, I decided that the best thing for me to do was to lay low and go out of my way not to be noticed. This had worked in my childhood, and it worked in the army too.

I came down with a terrible upper respiratory infection while training in the cold of winter but chose not to go on sick call because rumor had it that anyone that did would be recycled and would have to start basic training all over. I didn't think that Sgt. Dearing even noticed me until the night that we were to run the obstacle course, which was flooded, and we were expected to low crawl through it. At the last moment, Sgt. Dearing instructed me to go to the tent and stand fire watch. He had known all the time that I was sick and respected the fact that I chose to continue my duties instead of going to the dispensary. The break that he gave me that night was the difference between getting recycled or graduating with the rest of my platoon. I never said thank you, and I don't think that he expected me to either.

It was the last week of training, and that was over before I knew it. The eight weeks that I spent at basic training probably had more to do with the way I would see the world, through manhood, which is the formation of my way of thinking, than any member of my family. The training taught me how to be a man and how to act like one. To this day I feel that military service should be mandatory for every man and woman in America, but it's the going to war that I disagree with. Wars are so indifferent; they take the good along with the bad and very few have any logical reasoning behind them. I'm sorry to say that there will always be war as long as there are more than two humans on this earth. What a pity.

Immediately after completion of basic training, I was sent across the post to begin my advanced training at the clerical school. It was probably the most boring time of my life, but it only lasted three weeks before I was called into my instructor's office. I was given the option of signing up for flight operations specialist, and I was told that if I applied that I would receive new orders for a station in Fort Rucker, Alabama. If I was accepted for this training, I could expect some flight training along with weather forecasting and navigation techniques. For some reason this sort of thing appealed to me, and I could not see myself typing letters for three years, so I signed the papers. In a matter of days, I was holding my orders for a flight to Alabama. I was hoping to get a two-week leave before going to Alabama, but it was not to be, for I had to report by the following Monday, which gave me three days to travel.

Fort Rucker was entirely different from Fort Leonard Wood in that almost the entire post was involved with some type of aviation training. There were helicopters everywhere. I was promoted to private first class upon receiving my MAAG assignment, which I found meant Military Assistance and Advisory Group, and I was told that each and every person in my training class had been selected above many other applicants, and that made me wonder what Sgt. Dearing had written in my review papers. Whatever it was, it must have been good, because I could think of nothing out of the ordinary that I had done in high school. I thought that maybe I was selected because of my father's military record. It would always be a mystery to me as to why I was selected above others.

Right off the bat, the training interested me because we started with map reading and plotting. Within a week, I knew how to plot a course, had the beginnings of navigation and weather forecasting, had received an extensive course on radios and radio operation, and had received advanced training with weapons such as grenade launchers and the M-60 machine gun. I learned how to break down and clean pistols such as the .38-caliber revolver and the .45-caliber automatic. By the end of my eight weeks of training at Fort Rucker, I was feeling pretty good about myself and felt that I was as combat ready a troop as there ever was. It turned out that I was lucky to feel that way because on the beginning of the ninth week, I received orders for the Republic of Vietnam. I was also happy to see that I had received a two-week leave to go home before going overseas. I had been dreaming of seeing Penny Paluska every day for almost four months now, and believe me when I say that I needed to see her. I had been thinking hard about asking her to marry me.

For some reason, I hadn't received many letters from her in the last month or so, and I chalked it up to a busy class schedule. I knew that it couldn't be that she had found another boyfriend because I knew that she loved me and that she always would, just as I would always love her. I could hardly wait to get home to her and see how she liked the new me. I was a soldier now, and I looked like one. In just four days, I would be holding her in my arms, loving her and kissing her. It was almost more than I could stand.

The next day I was called before my commanding officer for a reason that I had not yet been informed of. All sorts of possible reasons ran wild through my little pea brain, and it was with great earnest that I finally stood before him. He seemed angry for some reason, and after a long five minutes or so of his sorting through papers, he asked, "Why didn't you inform us of your brother that is stationed in Vietnam with the Marine Corps?" I replied that I hadn't thought that it was important, to which he informed me that it was against regulations to have two brothers in the same combat zone. I didn't know that, so I asked if this was going to be a problem for me. He replied, "Not if you will sign this waiver form, waving your rights in this case, and then all will be copasetic."

"You bet I will, sir" was my instantaneous reply. He then asked me if I thought that my brother would also sign the form, and I told him, yes, I thought he would. Upon signing the form, I was dismissed and given a good-luck handshake by the Lt. Colonel, and then I was off to the barracks to pack my clothes for my trip home to Penny Paluska.

The flight home seemed to take forever, but my stepfather, Chuck, was standing there waiting for me at the airport. After a short greeting and his telling me how good I looked, I immediately asked him if I could use his car to go and see Penny. He instantly agreed and filled the car up with gas for me before giving me the keys once we arrived home. I kissed my mother, threw my bags on my old bed, and I was off to Penny's school. Down the road I flew, and I knew that with my stepfather's car I could cut the hour-and-a-half trip down to an hour. I was in a hurry to see my girl!

There were students everywhere, loading their belongings into cars and trucks for the trip home for the summer, and I hoped that Penny could go home with me. I parked as quickly as I could and ran to the high-rise dorm that Penny called home for the school year. In the lobby I used the desk phone to call her room to surprise her with my visit. She seemed very surprised indeed when I told her that I was in the lobby of her dorm and that I was going to give her a ride home. She told me that she would be right down, and I waited by the elevators to see her pretty face. When she emerged, it took my breath away to see how beautiful she had grown in the short time that I had been away. She had grown up too, and it looked good on her. She was simply lovely, and it did my heart good to see her. We sat and talked for a few minutes, exchanged a few peck kisses, and then I asked if I could take her home. She explained that she had already made plans to ride home with a friend's parents and they were going to stop and have dinner on the way, but she would be home the following day and we could be together then. She asked if I could take some of her belongings with me and drop them off at her mother's. "Certainly," I said, and I loaded them up and was off with a smile on my face because I knew that we would be together the next day.

I dropped her things off at her mother's, said hello to them, and then I was off to party with my friends. At this time there were no drugs in East Peoria to speak of, so it was all beer and shots of whiskey for my friends and me that night. The next morning I arose with a slight hangover, which was the norm during my youth. It was years later before the hangovers started hurting and lasting for days at a time. I was up and on the phone before eight that morning, and it was Penny's mother that answered the phone. "Is Penny up yet?" I asked. She seemed surprised that I didn't know that Penny wasn't coming home for a week or two. I told her that Penny had told me that she would be home late the previous night and for me to call her when I got up. Betty claimed ignorance of the whole situation, so I told her that I would call the school to check on Penny. That was the end of our conversation.

Penny's roommate, Bev Martini, was a former classmate of ours in high school, and we were close friends for several years. Bev answered the phone and told me that she had heard that I was home and was hoping to see me to say hello. When I asked for Penny, she hesitated for a long period of time before saying, "Don, I like you too much to lie to you, so I'm going to tell you the truth." When I asked what was wrong, she told me this story.

Penny had found someone new. She had fallen for a guy she met on campus. He was a former student at WIU, but he was now a roving hippie-type guy that hung around campus, mooching off the students, and selling drugs. She told me that Penny was using drugs and that she was infatuated with the new guy. She said that she was sorry but Penny didn't want to see me for a while and asked if I would please respect her wishes and not try to find her and cause her any problems. At this, I thanked Bev for her honesty and said that I would cause her no problems because I loved Penny very much, and I would never want to stop her from being happy. I thanked her again and hung up.

Again I felt that old familiar lump in my throat, and I could feel the tears trying to well up in my eyes. I had learned long ago how to control this, and as hard as it was not to cry, I succeeded in pushing them back one last time. All my dreams about the future were wiped out in one fell swoop. All my visions of Penny and me having children and growing old together were gone too. I thought to myself, "I'm glad I didn't buy a ring." All I had dreamed of seemed to float through my mind against my will, but I could not chase them away. They were too precious to me, too important to just let go, but that's exactly what I had to do: let them go. I stood up, brushed myself off, and began to prepare for war. It was too early to report to Oakland for transport overseas, so I just sat and talked with my mother and stepfather for the rest of the two weeks.

My mother and a friend of hers tried to set me up with a dinner date with the friend's daughter, a girl I had known in high school, although she was several classes behind me. I'd remembered how pretty she was, so I agreed to go out with her. The date was nice, and she was nice, but she wasn't Penny. I was as polite as I could be, but I told her that I was going away in a couple of days, so there was no reason to even try to like me because I was as good as gone. She told me that she had heard about Penny and that she had always thought that Penny and I would marry and be together forever. I said, "So did I." I paid the bill, thanked her for the date, and took her home. At the door, she gave me a warm kiss and told me to look her up when I got back home. I told her that I would do just that, and then I was gone.

Two days later I was standing in line to report for transportation to Vietnam, still trying to force Penny Paluska from my tormented mind. I found an empty bunk, laid down, and that's where I was two days later when they called my name. I was given a seat number and told to report at 1100 hours for transport. Within an hour I was issued jungle fatigues and jungle boots and all sorts of dark OD green shirts and underwear. As bright and green as these clothes were, there would be no mistake who the new guy was. It was me, and it wasn't pretty. 1100 hours came quickly, and I was surprised to find that instead of a military transport aircraft, we were to board a United Airlines 707. There would be an inflight movie, and we were treated like roy-alty, except for the no-alcohol rule. I had yearned for some alcohol for the last week or so, and I had even tried to buy some beer before leaving home, but I was carded and told to come back in two weeks when I would turn twenty-one. I told the clerk that I would be in Vietnam in two weeks, and all he could say was sorry. Anyway, the flight to Vietnam lasted for over twenty-one hours, with a one-hour layover at Honolulu, which was a treat for me because now I could claim to have been in Hawaii. The movie was a Dean Martin movie about a spy named Matt Helm. Kind of slow, but it was entertaining enough to pass several hours. Most of the time I spent with my headphones on, listen-ing to the radio, but every song seemed to remind me of Penny, so I could only take so much of that. I chatted with the guy in the next seat, but he was so dumb that I distinctly remember thinking that this guy was never going to make it. He gonna die right here in Vietnam.

That was when it hit me. I hadn't thought much about it before, but I did now. I was going to war, an obviously dangerous place, where people shoot at you and try to kill you. I began to look around the aircraft to see if I could pick out who was going to die and who was going to live. I found myself classifying men into categories of yes, no, and maybe. I kind of felt like God, because it never crossed my mind that I might die in Vietnam, not even once on the whole flight. Now that I think about it, there was only one of two times that I ever thought that I might die. This was gruesome thinking, but it helped me forget about Penny, who was forever creeping into my mind to rebreak my heart each time. I was really having a hard time with this, and it brought me back to when I had cut my wrist as a kid in the orphanage. I remember wishing that I had done the job correctly the first time. There was nothing I could do to keep her out, try as I may; it just could not be done. It was a living hell for me, and I didn't know what I could do to push the thoughts of her from my mind, but I had to try and keep trying for as long as it took.

Japan appeared out of the mist, and I could see Mt. Fuji from across the aisle window. I remember how beautiful it looked with its snow-covered top. I wished that Penny was there to see it too, and there it had happened again. She had walked right into my mind and sat down just like she owned the place. She must have owned my mind because she came and went whenever she pleased, without a hello or a good-bye. It was cruel, cruel and vicious, but I had to learn to live with it because I could not force her out. She was gone, and I could not bring her back. I wondered if others could see how much I was hurting if they looked into my eyes. I hoped not, but it was obvious to me every time I glanced into a mirror. It was there just below the surface, just out of sight. Sometimes it felt like an animal inside me that was tearing its way out, trying to get into the open air. It would take many months of hard work to get a grip on my grief over the loss of Penny Paluska, the girl I loved and always would love.

Five

Twenty-two and a half hours was the total time of the long flight, but finally Vietnam was in full view out of every window of the aircraft. It looked just like Oakland, but as we drew nearer and nearer, distinct differences became apparent. Motor bikes were the first thing I noticed, and they were everywhere. The military vehicles rivaled their numbers, followed by bicycles, millions of them, everywhere you looked. Once we flew over the line that divided the military compound from city, the vehicles grew larger and more menacing. Some had fifty-caliber machine guns and a few had even bigger ones. I thought about it for a moment, and I figured that this would never end; the guns would get bigger and bigger until they killed us all. At long last, the wheels of the jet touched the ground with a screech, and I had arrived at the war. I looked out the window but could see nothing out of the ordinary. Nothing that couldn't be seen on any military compound in the United States, except a sort of smog that hung low over what I took to be a city in the distance. The big jet taxied in and came to a stop. I could see some Asian men pushing a set of rolling stairs up to the side of the aircraft. With a sudden whoosh, the aircraft doors were opened, which let the cool air conditioning out and a sudden blast of hot, humid air in that rushed to hit me square in the face. It was hot. Hot air that was fragrant with the odors of foreign and exotic places. The prevailing odor, I found, would be the same everywhere I went in Vietnam. It was the odor of Nuk Mom; the smell of the sauce that the Vietnamese cooks put on all their food. I was told that it was the product of a process of squeezing the juice out of rotten fish. I believed it at first because it did resemble the smell of rotten fish, carp in particular.

I could see smoke off in the distance, but I couldn't tell what had caused it. I imagined that it was caused by some gruesome battle in which many had died, and the smoke was from their funeral pyre. With the terminal stairs in front of me, I was forced back to where I was. As I walked down the stairs and into the terminal building, I noticed that the Vietnamese were everywhere, and I began to wonder how the hell I could tell the good ones from the bad ones, the friend from the foe. I resolved that the bad ones would be trying to kill me, so that gave me an obvious answer. The good ones would not try to kill me. Inside the terminal, a kid who had to be around sixteen checked my orders, and I thought how obvious it was to me that he had lied about his age to get into the army. He pointed to a row of benches and told me to sit and wait and eventually someone would arrive to transport me to the headquarters company of the 1st Aviation Brigade, and he was right because it was only two hours before another asshole arrived, and he too checked my orders and told me to board the bus outside and not to wander off until he could come up with a full load of people. Four hours later, there were six of us on the bus, and finally the second asshole showed up and started the bus. A short ten-minute ride and my orders were checked a third time, this time at MACV Headquarters in Ben Hoa, home of the 1st Aviation Brigade, and I was told to find an empty hooch, flop into the first empty bunk that I could find, and that the time was all mine except for formations that were held in the yard twice daily. I was to attend each formation until my name was called for assignment to my next post. It was a long, boring wait.

Three days later my orders arrived. I had been assigned to the 268th Aviation Battalion at Phu Hiep, a dot on the map somewhere in the central highlands above Nha Trang. I was driven to a landing pad at Ben Hoa Army Air Field, where I was spirited aboard a UH-1D Huey helicopter for the flight to Phu Hiep. This was to be my first helicopter ride, and it was truly magnificent. What a wonderful invention, the helicopter. The power at liftoff was the most exhilarating thing that I had ever felt since I was still a virgin and had to exclude sex. I enjoyed the ride over the rice fields, the jungles, and the mountains on high. All were so beautiful from the air. The wind rushed through the aircraft's open doors, and the higher we climbed, the cooler it got. It was so beautiful that I instantly fell in love with Vietnam. Despite the obvious war damage, it was so beautiful, a paradise. It was beyond me how anybody in his right mind could pockmark this beautiful country with so many bomb craters, scarifying such a lush and lively countryside. I knew so little about it, and I hungered to know more. Most highways were two lanes wide, but there was a two-hundred-foot swath cut through the foliage on either side of each road. The only thing that I knew for certain at this point was that I was in a helicopter flying over what could be hostile country, and I hadn't even been issued a weapon. I looked around the chopper, taking note of where each weapon was in case I had to take one. The pilot and the copilot each had .38-caliber pistols, and the gunner and crew chief each had .45-caliber pistols and an M-60 machine gun with aviation grips. The crew chief was nearest to me, so I figured that if I had to have one, I would take his pistol. I tried to figure out why more of these choppers weren't shot down. One round in the transmission or in the hydraulics, and down it would go, hard. It seems to me that it could be done so easily by just one man with a rifle. Hard thinking, but at least I wasn't thinking of Penny Paluska.

The crew chief nudged me and pointed toward a small shiny airstrip made up of pieced-together strips of steel PSP, as it was called. He smiled at me and said, "Home, Phu Hiep." The whole compound would probably fit into five football fields; there was the small strip with a maintenance hangar, about ten rows of buildings that I could only guess were the barracks, and twenty or thirty helicopters of different types. At one end stood the largest, which I recognized as Chinooks, or CH-47s. In the middle were the UH-1 Hueys, and at the far end were the Cobra Gun Ships, which I hoped that I would be assigned to, for they were sleek and beautiful killing machines. We landed near the other Hueys, and for the first time, I noticed that the numbers and emblems were the same as the rest of the Hueys. This chopper belonged to the 134th Assault Helicopter Company, and I thanked the pilot for the ride, before reporting to the company clerk at headquarters, 268th Aviation Battalion Av. Bt. Again I was told to grab an empty bunk in the transit barracks, attend the formations, and not to wander to far, which was impossible because I could walk around the entire compound in fifteen minutes. Eight-foot high consentena wire fences, enclosed a minefield, and another eight-foot fence on the outside surrounded the entire compound. Two guarded gates were the only way in or out, unless it was by air. The mine fields were criss crossed with paths that cut across from here to there, which made me wonder if there were really any explosives there at all. Eventually, I found a sign that said, "EM Club," and I made a beeline for the entrance, but found it was closed until 1600 hours. That evening, I could hardly wait. Eventually it did open, and I entered to find that the room was racially segregated. On one side were the whites, and on the other side, the blacks. Some of the soldiers looked pretty rough, and I made a point not to rub anybody the wrong way. Some of the blacks wore headbands, beaded necklaces, and chain bracelets that I later found were made of the timing chains from the helicopters. I drank my fill of beer, served in cans that were faded, as if they had lain in the sun for a long period of time. When opened, the first can was flat, and the bartender immediately replaced it. By 2200 hours, I was feeling no pain and made my way back to my bunk, where I went out like a light.

At formation the following morning, I was told to report to the company clerk after chow. It was a few minutes before I remembered that it was my twenty-first birthday. "Happy birthday to me," I said. Then I took my choice of the three chow halls on the compound, ate what turned out to be a very good breakfast, and then made my way to the company clerk, who had just dittoed my orders, apparently, because they were still wet and smelled of the printing ink. "It's the 180th for you," he said. And he sent me on my way down the dirt road, carrying my duffel bag on my shoulder toward the 180th Assault Support Helicopter Company (ASHC).

It took me all of five minutes to walk the distance from battalion to the 180th commander's office, where I reported to the first sergeant, as he was the only person in sight. He introduced himself and directed me to operations, which happened to be in the rear of the same building. There, I was introduced to the operations officer that went by the name of Captain Gary Cooper, a tall, thin, red-headed cowboy from Oklahoma. He in turn gave me over to the operations sergeant, an E-7 that was named Batten. They gave me a day to get settled in and told me to report for work on the following morning.

The sergeant walked me down a metal sidewalk, past several barracks that had ten rooms, each divided into four hooches. The shitter, a twenty-holer, and a six-stall shower, stood near, but it only had cold water. I was taken to a temporary bunk because the man whom I was to replace was not to leave for at least a week, and when he did leave, I was assured his hooch.

Everything seemed really relaxed and calm and pretty laid back. The bunk that I was given was centered between two men who worked at the POL, or fuel dump, so of course the whole room reeked of aviation fuel. The very first thing that came out of their mouths was an order for me to get the fuck outta their hooch, which I started to do, until they started to laugh and told me that they were only joking. One of them, the biggest, was named Charles Shultz, from Cincinnati, Ohio. He was a fat, jolly, and kind-mannered man who would befriend me, and we would remain friends until the day that he went home. The other man was an aircraft gunner named Frenchy LaChance. He too was a friend, and we were so close that he would let me read his letters and showed me the pictures of his naked wife, which I truly appreciated. Frenchy was a Canadian citizen that was attending a college in the United States and was drafted. This was completely legal, as he assured me, because the FBI had to arrest him and taken him to Fort Meade, Maryland, for induction into the army. He was trained as a LRRP (long range reconnaissance patrol) but finagled his way into the aircraft gunnery business, as he liked to say. I enjoyed the time that I shared with them in their hooch, and I learned a lot about fuel and shooting an M-60 from a moving helicopter. I borrowed some stationary from them and fired a letter to my brother, informing him of my in-country arrival. I received a reply within three weeks informing me that he had not signed the waiver and was in turn removed from the combat zone and sent to Okinawa, Japan, to be returned to a combat assignment upon the completion of my tour of duty in Vietnam. I was amazed at the speed with which he was removed from the combat zone but was truly grateful that he had made it out alive and well.

That evening I helped fill sandbags to rebuild a collapsed bunker, and while doing so, I met more men of the 180th, and I can truly say that I was made to feel right at home, and I even got to use one of three shovels, which, as we all knew, was a real privilege. The man whom I was to replace arrived on the first homecoming Chinook chopper and swirled in at a frantic pace, screaming, "Short!" This was local lingo for "Ready to go home?" He introduced me to the other three men I was to share hooches with upon his departure. Martinez, Scott, and Woody were the men I was to live with until I saw them all go home, one at a time. I found that there was a stocked bar in our hooch, and we were to make good use of it in the near future. I told them that I liked the string beads that hung in the doorway in place of a door. There was a four-foot revetment that completely encircled the hooches that would provide some protection in the event of an enemy mortar attack. Above the revetment were rows of screened-in windows that contained no glass because of the hot weather. I seemed to fit right in and soon started to relax and feel comfortable enough to ask any question that I didn't think was too stupid.

The next morning after chow, I reported to operations to begin working, and I was eager to start because it was the only way to make the time pass. I was broken in on the radio, and soon was the preferred operator because I had been trained on the proper use and procedures, and at first I went by the book any time that I used it. After a while, I relaxed and used the same techniques that everybody else used. I worked with the operations officer assigning crews and receiving sortie information and requests from the units that we were to support. It took a while for me to fully understand the lingo of combat operations, but slowly I gained a full command of all the many functions of the operations of the 180th. I finally received a rifle that day, and it was my favorite weapon, an M-14. I think that it is one of the best rifles ever made. I loved it. On the second day, I was told that if I wanted to go to the PX, there was a truck leaving for Tuy Hoa Air force Base, and I could accompany them if I wished. I jumped at the chance, and I was off on my first adventure outside the fences of Phu Hiep. There were eight of us in the three-quarter-ton truck, followed by two more in a jeep, with an M-60 machine gun mounted on it. We drove down a two-lane road that was crowded with Vietnamese walking either way on the side of the road. Military vehicles crowded the road, and I could see that some were South Vietnamese or, ARVN, and some were Korean. Through small villages, over damaged bridges, and around checkpoints we went, until we reached a city that I was told was Tuy Hoa, which is pronounced too-*E-WAH*. The Vietnamese city fascinated me, and I couldn't wait to explore it when I got the time. We arrived at the air force base about half an hour after passing the city of Tuy Hoa, and I was surprised at how modern and organized it was for a war zone. The PX was small but had everything that I needed. Cartons of cigarettes were two dollars a carton, but they only had Camels. Coke and beer were about the same price but was hot and had been stored in the sun for who knows how long, hence the faded cans that I had encountered at the EM club. I bought a little tape recorder and player so that I could record and receive tapes for home. Woody gave me Steppenwolf and Santana tapes before he went home, so I had all the music that I needed.

I was delighted to learn that we had a maid, a pretty little Vietnamese girl named Kim Truk. Each of us paid her about five dollars a month to wash all of our clothes and clean our hooch, and although she was about our age, she treated us like a mother would treat her sons. Most hooch maids were respectable women who stood for no hanky-panky of any sort.

Throwing a pass at a hooch maid could cause a world of trouble. Say the wrong thing, and they would run through the compound screaming and yakking at the top of their lungs, stirring up every other hooch maid on the compound. Oh, it was horrible thing to behold. The racket was unbearable, and when one was unhappy, they all were. Life in general would be unbearable for all. As a group they had considerable power, and they had many friends in high places. The first time that I witnessed this event, I thought that someone had been killed. There was a loud wailing and chatter that no one could understand, as loud as a loudspeaker.

I think that Kim must have been about eighteen years old when I first met her because she giggled a lot with her friends and told me that I was bookoo dep, which means very handsome. I was fond of her, and she was fond of me too, and I always would overpay her. When she got married, she invited me to attend the wedding, but due to a radical increase in enemy activity in the Tuy Hoa area, I was denied permission to attend by my commanding officer. I gave them a nice sum of money as a wedding present, and I always appreciated the way she took care of me.

After a while in-country, several new guys came in, so I therefore was no longer the FNG (fucking new guy). I found that the longer you have been in-country, the harder life becomes, not in a normal way, but in ways that are common only to war zones. Eventually, if you live long enough, you will encounter the enemy, both dead and alive (preferably dead), your life will be threatened, and sooner or later a fear that you can't control will grasp you around the neck and shake you within an inch of your life. Another common thing that I think is the hardest to take is the death or injury of a friend or acquaintance. There is nothing worse than the helpless feeling that comes along with injuries sustained as a result of combat. I was just a kid when I got to Vietnam, and the first time I saw a dead enemy soldier, I got sick. It was just luck, I guess, because the first time that I saw a dead Viet Cong, there was six of them all laid out in a row in front of headquarters, placed there specifically for the purpose of everyone's picture outings. At first, it shocked me, but as time passed I warmed up to the idea and took some pictures of my own. One picture that stands out in my mind was when I stood with my foot on a dead VC while I proudly held my rifle like I had just shot a tiger. If you live long enough in Vietnam, you will be reprogrammed to think and act in a manner that is common to most combat veterans: you become hardened to the world and have absolutely no respect for the dead.

I don't want to get carried away with talk such as this, for it is a private thing for me and me alone to have to live with the way that I have acted in the past. It's hard for me to face it for myself, and I don't want anyone to ever know that I was like that and that I was a different person, a cruel person, that picked up evil ways from an evil war. I wish that things had been different, but they weren't, so it's for me and me alone to remember the good things and forget the bad things if I can. I had given up on God many years before, and that left me with nothing and no one to fall back on. It's a shame, but that's the way it was, and I can't change a thing, not even one little thing. This story is becoming very hard for me to relay to you, but I am going to continue because I think that it's important to get it out from where it's trapped, deep inside of me and other Vietnam vets that are just like me.

In my adult life I have always tried to treat others with kindness and respect, and I always demanded the same from them and usually got it. I have found that, even people of other cultures know when they are treated with respect, and it's all that's needed to communicate in any language, in any land, far or near. An enemy soldier, unless he is filled with hate and revenge, does not want to meet you in battle, and I am the same. I would rather have a picnic than a fight, and I will usually bend over backward to get it that way. For me, the world has always been a hard place, and in return I tried to make it hard for others, but I found that it doesn't work that way because while you're making it hard for them, you're making it hard for you too. That is not a good thing; believe me.

All of these feelings and many more streamed through my body as I stood looking down at the dead soldiers. What horrified me the most was the total lack of respect that was shown to those brave soldiers that fought and died while facing incredible odds. The American fighting machine is an awesome thing. To take a stand against such a force must take something that has eluded me, for I don't know what it is or even what to call it. I only know that the Vietnamese soldier is by far the toughest son of a bitch that ever lived, and I will feel that way until the day I die. I got sick at the sight of them and the lack of respect, but eventually something wore me down. I don't know what it was, and I have no name for it either, but I know that it is real. It can't be seen, only felt after the fact.

After this first encounter with the enemy, I was a changed man, for I had finally seen, with my own eyes, the end result of war. Although the sight of it sickened me, I could not divert my eyes from the horrible sight. I had seen what my father must have seen, and his father before him. I'm trying to put into words something that can't be described, only experienced. For all that I am, I truly wished that I would never have to see the face of war again, but I had just arrived in Vietnam, and I had almost an entire tour of duty yet to serve, and I knew in my heart that it could not be avoided. I knew I must harden myself as I had never had to harden myself before, and I must do it soon. I had to learn some way, somehow, something to help me keep it from driving me crazy. I couldn't let it bother me as it had before. I think that most soldiers handle it by dehumanizing the enemy. After all, they were just gooks or dirty yellow dogs, whatever, but it became imperative to me not to see them as human, and that I could not handle. For some reason I kept this all to myself and never mentioned it to anyone for fear of being thought weak. I kept it inside, where it began to fester and infect my spirit. I think that is a good description of how I was feeling at the time. My spirit was not dead, but it was certainly sick.

I found myself wanting to learn more about my enemy, and I read any document that I could get my hands on. I was given a security clearance of SECRET, and it was part of my duties to pick up classified material from the COMO, or communications station, and transport it to the hands of whoever was intended to receive it. I was not allowed to read or even look at secret documents unless it was decided that I had a need to know, as they say. It was usually decided that I should know what was going on because I was the only operations specialist in the company and one of only four in the whole battalion. Sometimes it nearly drove me crazy when I knew something but couldn't tell anyone else. I have never been good at keeping secrets, but now I had to under penalty of law. It was almost too much for me at times. When we received the new scramblers for our radios, it was my duty to set the secret codes into the little machines and hand them out to each pilot every morning and to collect them and lock them up at night. For the most part, I enjoyed this part of my job, but it required a lot of hours to do it. What the hell—there wasn't a damn thing else to do.

In time, my job became almost boring, so I started to go along on missions if I thought they might be interesting. I had a hand in the assignment of the missions, so I knew which ones were good and which ones were going to be boring. Combat troop insertions were the ones that excited me and made me feel alive. Another one that I really liked was the transportation of entertainment personnel and the beautiful women who were involved with the shows. We would fly them from firebase to firebase, and I could enjoy the shows over and over with the added benefit of socializing with the entertainers while in transport. I was always interested when an aircraft was to go to a part of the country that I hadn't seen or if they were to go to Saigon or Cam Ron Bay. They were always fun to go on. I was particularly interested in missions in support of the White Horse Division of the ROK (Republic of Korea) Army, for they always seemed to be where the action was; if not, they would create their own. They were splendid soldiers, very polite, and they would always treat me as was one of their officers, sometimes inviting me to meals with their commander. I had a real respect for the Korean soldier, for they were truly as near to the perfect soldier as you will ever see. They were taught to obey any order without question. While on these missions, I would always return to Phu Hiep in the evening, for it would take a tactical emergency for a Chinook helicopter to be flown at night, and that was not the norm.

It was on one of the missions in support of the ROK White Horse Division that I witnessed the killing of a South Vietnamese civilian at the hands of a Korean captain, or daiwi, as they are called. I never knew the reason for the killing, and I didn't think it wise to ask questions about it, but it did have an effect on me, probably negative.

At that point, death was becoming a common occurrence in my life, and when I think back on the killing, I was no more horrified than at the sight of a man who was already dead. I would have thought that actually seeing someone die and maybe feeling his spirit rise up out of his body would have had a much more traumatic effect, but it didn't.

I had seen the captain pull his pistol and point it at the man, but before I could turn away, he had fired the gun, and the man fell like a sack of potatoes. Something was mentioned about the rape of a young boy, but it was never clarified, and I didn't ask. The thing that really frightened me was the fact that the next time I might not try to look away. I reported the incident to Captain Cooper, and although he thought it was interesting, he didn't think that it was worth mention in the mission report. What I neglected to tell him was the fact that I had passed out cold and awakened later in a gazebo where the Korean Captain was sipping tea with his commander, and they smiled at me when I awoke.

Other missions in support of the White Horse Division were just as exciting, and dangerous. Operation Doksgoori (eagle) was a mass troop insertion into the mountains near Tuy Hoa that was supposed to encounter at least one thousand enemy troops that were dug in and part of a major communist buildup. We made five sorties, each one carrying thirty Korean troops to a variety of different landing zones LZs that were all supposed to be hot and were marked by red smoke. Wounded ROK troops were medevacked on two of the return trips, which was my first clue that this was a real game this time. It was not just another useless attempt at catching the enemy. So many of the other missions turned out that way and were a major disappointment to me. At the end of the day, there was actually a number of enemy dead lined up at the main LZ for everyone to photograph. Several weeks later, there was an article in the *Army Times* that described the operation, so I cut it out and saved it and put it in this book.

The work that I was doing was becoming a boring routine for me, and I remember wishing that something would happen to liven things up, and it wasn't long before my wish came true. On one of my trips to the COMO, I picked up a confidential report stating that the 180th ASHC was to move in and effectively provide air support for the area centered at Ple Ku. That area was previously supported by our sister company, the 196th ASHC, which was now ordered north to support the area centered at Da Nang—an area which was previously supported by the US Marine Corps. The report also informed all readers that the 1st Marine Division was to be extracted as a unit and moved to the island of Okinawa, Japan, for eventual transport to US soil. Anyway, the main point of the communication for me was that the 180th was to move part of its operation to Ple Ku in support of the 173rd Infantry Division, whom we were already supporting out of LZ English further to the east.

I was allowed to sit in on the planning of how this operation was to establish a new center of operation that would be separate but still under control of operations at Phu Hiep. I was elected to run mobile ops, meaning that I was to report by landline, on a daily basis, and I would move my mobile ops to Ple Ku. I was to receive an early promotion to Specialist-4, and I was assigned a jeep equipped with both regular and Fox Mike radios. I was told that I had better sleep in this jeep, for it would be my ass if it came up missing. This move was to occur no later than the end of the month and no earlier than a week. It took me every bit of that time to get established and move everything to Ple Ku, along with three of our aircraft that would be temporarily stationed there.

When I arrived in Ple Ku, I found it practically deserted, and I had an entire building to myself, which would accommodate me and my jeep, which I drove right inside and parked near my bunk. If I had known how boring it would be, I would have begged to stay at Phu Hiep. From the time of liftoff of the first sortie until the return of the aircraft at the end of the day, I had absolutely nothing to do. I mean nothing. I couldn't leave my radios without security, and there was no PX, so I sat on my ass and prayed to have an end to this operation so that I could return to my other, not-as-boring-but-still-boring job in Phu Hiep. Two things about my stay in Ple Ku worth mentioning are the red dirt that turned everything red on contact and the huge lizard that was brought in from the jungle by some grunt. As he held the dead lizard at arm's length above his head, the lizard's tail touched the ground. That was some lizard! Oh yes, I forgot about the elephants that looked pink after rolling in the red Ple Ku dirt. Everything, I mean everything else was a total and complete bore. I was never as happy as when the area was taken over by ARVN troops.

Buddhist temples that were thousands and thousands of years old dotted the countryside throughout Vietnam. One of these ancient pagodas we used as target practice. As our aircraft would circle around the temple, the gunners and I would take turns using the pagoda to practice our aerial gunnery. Firing from a moving helicopter, I found, was a very tricky thing to do, and I could not hit a thing, even if I'd paid them to stand still. As a rule, you have to fire forward of the target, and if you watch the tracer rounds, they would travel in an *S*-shaped trajectory. It was the strangest thing to me, and I don't know how the gunners could hit anything, but they did. Later in my tour of duty in Vietnam, I got the distinct feeling that Buddha was mad at me and was laying his revenge on me. I will tell the reason for this feeling in full in later pages.

Another thing that I participated in was the US policy of body count. I was instructed to complete a weekly form to be sent to operations, which concerned the number of enemy that were KIA as a direct result of our operations. I would always beef up the report, as I was unofficially instructed to do by my commanding officer. I thought that the only person who would want information like that had to be some sick politician that got off on such things. Anyway, this form had negative backlash for me, and I wish that I had never heard of body count. I read somewhere, years later, that over one million VC and NVA soldiers were KIA, at a cost of almost ten thousand dollars a head. If you could stack up all the dead Vietnamese, the pile would reach clear out into outer space.

I can remember sitting on the canvas bench in a Chinook, and at my feet were twenty or so dead South Vietnamese soldiers, half-covered by ponchos or field jackets. When I think about it now, it really freaks me out, but at the time it just seemed like business. I guess if I had been a God-fearing human being, I would have checked the pulse of each soldier. For some reason, I just sat there looking dumber than a sack of shit. I have no idea where my mind was at. I really did some stupid shit in those days. God, I was so stupid. Sometimes I amaze myself.

One night one of the bridges that had to be crossed to get to Tuy Hoa Air Force Base was blown sky high. One day it was there, and the next it was gone. The VC floated a large bomb down the river and detonated it at the center span of the bridge. The whole span collapsed into the river, forcing all traffic to use the old railroad bridge that stood adjacent to it. I guess the VC thought it a kind of joke, but the locals didn't seem to think so, and when the town elders spoke out against it, they were all murdered and hung from the old bridge. I wanted a picture, but the bodies were removed before I could get there.

I was still a virgin, all the way until the middle of my twenty-first year, so I jumped at the chance when I was told that there was a whore in Frenchy's hooch that was going for two dollars a pop. The line was only three people deep, so I stood there and waited until it was my turn. Upon entering the room, there she was, naked as a jaybird, squatting over a bucket of water and, I suppose, washing off her private parts. She wasn't very appetizing, but by God, I was a virgin and it was high time that it ended. Unabashedly she lay on the bed with her legs spread, with a look on her face like she was bored with the whole show, but I didn't care, so I just climbed on, did my thing, and climbed off just like that. It wasn't a week or two later that I came down with a whopping case of the clap! I'm afraid that my first sexual encounter was nothing to brag about.

I was too young and dumb at the time to even think about her or her feelings. What must she have thought of me? Was she afraid of me? Was she being forced into her situation? I will never really know, but I suspect that probably she did not have a choice in the matter. I think that she probably never had a man who would truly love her. A man who would give her what she wanted to meet her needs. I suspect that her lifestyle eventually killed her and that she never truly reached happiness. Now I would like to tell her that I am sorry and that I cry for her and what I did to her. I am ashamed of my behavior toward her. It never dawned on me that she might not want me there. I was so stupid; I treated her like she was nothing more than an animal. I wish that I could change many things that I have done in my life, some small and some large. This one event is as close to the top of the list as it can get without crowding everything else off the list.

Within a couple of months, I had caught two more cases of VD, and that's the way it went for me. Before I would leave Vietnam, I would have five more good cases of the clap. This, I was told, was the company record for the most cases of VD. Maybe it was a record for the entire country; I don't know. My first year in Vietnam was almost over, and I had applied for and received a six-month extension that entitled me to remain in-country for another six months. I took a seven-day leave to Hawaii that started out bad, was boring, and ended up worse. When the jet landed in Hawaii, and we all left the aircraft, we walked between double rows of women who all looked and smelled so good to me. They were all standing there waiting and looking for their men. I looked at each and every one of them, hoping to see Penny Paluska, but by the time I got to the end of the line, I was alone. Everyone else had someone there to meet them. I felt so bad and alone at that moment that it ruined my whole R and R. I talked only briefly to a bartender, the hotel clerk, and a rental-car representative. On the first day, I couldn't wait until my R and R was over. I wished that I could get back to Vietnam so bad, and those seven days were the longest of my life.

Several months later, I took a seven-day R and R to Bangkok, Thailand. Now, this was a different story altogether. Bangkok was a beautiful place to visit, and in the next year, I would return four more times. In Bangkok I was treated like royalty, and at a rate that I could really afford. The rooms, the drivers that were at your beck and call twenty-four hours a day, and the cheapest and most beautiful whores in the world all combined to make it a most pleasurable event for me.

I mean to tell you that these were world-class whores. Some were really beautiful, and the good thing was that the pretty ones were just as cheap as the ugly ones. Eventually the pretty whores got so boring that I took some ugly ones just for a change of pace.

One of them took me to meet her parents. I thought this was odd, but I found her family warm and welcoming. My driver told me that I was the first person their daughter had brought into their home. The reason for the visit was that her older brother had just come home after spending a year roaming the country as a Buddhist monk. I guess it is tradition for every male child to spend a year with the monks, begging for their food from strangers. This, I understood, would teach them about humility and generosity and leave them with a giving nature. I had an excellent time at their home. It was set right on the swirling brown river that was like the vein from the hand to the heart. That river was a highway, a market, a swimming hole, and a bath. From this river, God furnished the water to wash, cook, and clean themselves and their homes.

Every trip to Bangkok was great, except for the last, which was kind of traumatic because the MPs picked me up and took me to the local military hospital for observation. By this time I was pretty fucked up, suicidal, and prone to displays of recklessness shadowed by moments of complete despair. I don't remember what it was that I did, but I must have made some sort of public display that made the MPs think that something was very wrong with me. That was the end of my R and Rs, and after several days of observation in the mental ward, I was put on a plane and sent back to Phu Hiep. The dumbasses gave me my medical records to carry back to battalion HQ, but I shitcanned them as soon as I was out of their sight. I did the same thing with my medical records and anything else that I didn't like when I carried my records back to the States when I went home. For some unknown reason, I didn't want anyone at home to realize what a nutcase I really was, and it would be many years before anyone found out.

Going back a few months, at the end of my first year, I received a thirty-day leave with orders to go home to East Peoria. It was on this leave that I heard about the shootings at Kent State. I was so upset by this event that I completely broke down and lost the rest of what little faith that remained in me for the government of the United States. I began to wonder why the hell we were fighting for our freedom when it was apparent that we were not free at all. I freaked out and I completely lost any faith that I had left. On top of that, everything, I mean everything, had changed at home. In one short year, everything was completely different. Everybody that I had once known had now become a hippie. I had no idea what the hell anyone was talking about. They had a completely new language. With my short hair and military manner, I fit like a square peg in a round hole. The drug scene was everywhere. Everybody had long hair. Worst of all, soldiers (particularly Vietnam soldiers) were felt to be and treated as the assholes of the universe. Vets were liable to be spit upon and cursed at, just for the simple fact that they were soldiers. It was at this time, my first day home, that I used drugs for the first time. I liked it. No, I loved it. It wasn't long before I was eating LSD like candy. I began thinking of going AWOL and never returning to Vietnam, but this would be desertion at a time of war, which carried some stiff penalties. One night I bumped into Penny Paluska at the local McDonald's, and surprisingly, it meant absolutely nothing to me. I said hello to her as I sat on a concrete bench with my elbows on my knees. She said, "Is that all you have to say?" I asked her what she wanted me to say, which I think insulted her because she dropped the whole thing right there and wandered off with her new friends. I wanted to go after her, but I didn't. Penny Paluska was all that I cared about in this world, but I was returning to Vietnam within a week or two, so why should I get her involved with all of my shit? I looked around, but she was gone. I was gone too; I was a goner, and I didn't even know it.

It was no real chore for me to return to the service, and upon arrival at Oakland for transport overseas, I was so high. I was really one fucked-up individual. When I put on my old faded fatigues, they were bleached almost white from the hot Vietnamese sun. I noticed how bright green everyone else's were. I kept pretty much to myself on the long flight back to Nam, as it was now called. The States had the nickname the world. "I'm going back to the world," they would say. Again, on the flight over, I tried to pick out the ones that were bound to die. It had become easier for me. When I got back to my unit, I told my friends about what was going on "back on the block." I think that was the expression. They called me a liar. It was unbelievable to them that the American people would spit on its returning soldiers. It was very, very sad, but it was true. They just could not believe it! They didn't want to.

I don't know what I expected, but my second tour in-country changed for the worse. I say that things got worse because we began to lose choppers and men at an alarming rate. We were a small company, 180 men and ten or twelve choppers, not counting the ones that were down for maintenance (scavenged for parts). One minute they were there, and the next they're smoke rising up in the air, swirling and swirling as the wind took it ever skyward until it disappeared from view. Most aircraft accidents were exactly that: accidents. I can tell you about three right off the top of my head. One happened so close to the operations office that the front window was blown out by the concussion. It had killed our maintenance officer, Chief Warrant Officer 2 CW2 Jacinski, SP4Specialist 4th class Ell, the flight engineer that was seated in the copilot's seat, and PFCPrivate First Class Duncan that was on the ramp. Their prop hit a revetment, causing the aircraft to climb vertically, invert, and then vibrate apart before falling and exploding into a ball of flames upon impact. Within weeks we lost Captains Straw and Ward to a midair collision at LZ English, along with SP5s Specialist 5 Dennison and Prentice and their gunner, SP4 Rayburn. CWO2 Robert Meade was killed within weeks of that accident, followed by PFC Valdez, who caught fire at our POL (fuel) station. Valdez was a Mexican from San Antonio who could throw a baseball so fast that no one could catch it. No one even wanted to try. Once he suckered me into catching for him before I found out how hard he could throw. I have played a lot of sandlot baseball, but I've never encountered anything like that before. He scared the holy shit right out of me on the first pitch, but I did catch it. The second was worse than the first because it curved, and I only had a flash to chase it before it hit me square in the balls. I caught that one too, thank God, but that was the last attempt that I made to catch anything from him. He was disappointed when I quit and walked off. He said that he would slow it down. I think that I told him that I'd rather he kiss my ass first before I'd catch another one; he laughed at that. They said that when Valdez caught fire, he ran down the metal runway screaming something in Spanish, until the flames took him down and he fell onto his knees, dead. Another chopper was pulled down into the trees when its sling load snagged in the treetops at liftoff. This last chopper was flying at night on a TAC-E (tactical emergency). I found out later that they were hauling garbage cans and some other worthless crap that was not worth dying for. It pissed me off.

I would see these people every day in ops before they were killed, and I'll be damned if I could remember what even one of them looked like. It's almost as if my brain would shut down to black them out, never to visualize what they looked like again. This was probably a good thing, but it still didn't help matters much. John Mac Masters was a different story altogether. He was kind of a greasy red-headed guy that slithered around the compound. I can't even remember what kind of job he had, but he thought he was a gambler, a real card shark. Apparently he bet against the wrong man or he got caught cheating, I don't know, but someone crushed his skull with a rifle butt. He was found near the wire the following morning, his pockets pulled inside out. I didn't care much for him, but I would never wish that on anybody. Then there was PFC Corcoran, a black man from Virginia, I think, who had watched the whores creep in and out of the compound, right through the mine field, and he thought that he could do it too, for some ungodly reason. Before he knew it, both of his feet and all the meat (including his genitals) between his legs were blown sky high. He got up, and actually walked on the bloody stubs before bleeding to death and collapsing. One after another they fell, I had to force myself to just let it pass and not think about it, or it would have driven me insane.

An interesting mission came up that I wanted to go on that involved the dropping of a chemical agent called phoo-gas onto some NVA bunkers. We were in support of the 51st Chemical Detachment. of the 173rd Airborne Brigade on an assault on the mountains near Tuy Hoa, in Phu Yen Province, east of the air force base. The mission involved the hauling of the chemical phoo-gas, carried in sling loads under our Chinook helicopters. We would punch the load onto the marked positions, supposedly the openings of the NVA tunnel complexes. Time was given for the gas to seep down into the tunnels, for this gas was heavier than air. After a short time, the gas was then ignited by the use of tracers from a Huey gunship. Of course it was my job to keep a running count of crispy critters, as they were called. The gas created a beautiful fireworks display that could be seen miles away in Phu Hiep. Later that week, I was told to adjust my tally of enemy KIAs. Because Vietnamese women who were KIA were now to be listed as simply "enemy KIA," I was no longer to distinguish gender as I had been accustomed to doing. I felt like asking how I should list the enemy that was under sixteen years of age, but I decided against it.

I used to enjoy watching the firing of the artillery pieces; I think it was like a phallic symbol that contained such awesome power when it blew. It reminded me of an orchestrated dance as I would watch the way the gun crew would load, fire, eject the spent casing, and then load again, all within a minute. I was amazed at how fast the big, spent, shell casings would be thrown into huge piles, each casing representing one dead "gook." I imagine that the remains of the enemy would fit nicely into that casing and buried, so that they would serve a dual purpose. I decided to keep that idea to myself too, when I thought, "Boy, my mind is slipping into some kind of sick perversion when it comes to the Vietnamese." I wondered how many other of my brother soldiers thought like that too. Then I saw the big and the small of it as I saw the officer in command of the firebase wringing his hands and smiling as he watched the fire mission wind down and the pieces finally became silent. It dawned on me that he was getting off on it, and I hoped that his excitement was centered on this end of the firing and not the other far away, bloody end. I hoped that he was like me, loving the noise and excitement while detesting the killing.

My ears would hurt sometimes from all the noise, and the pain would increase through the years until near the end of my last tour, when they started to seep blood. With this, my hearing gradually got worse and worse, and I could tell that I would have trouble with it in the future, if I lived through all this shit. I know that the high-pitched whine of the turbine engines must have shredded my eardrums, and when I look back on it, we had no protection other than the flight helmets that were a poor fit around the ears, or at least mine was. It seems that people never worry about such things until the damage is done, but in a military situation, if you complain about anything, you might as well bend over and kiss your ass good-bye, I can't say that this policy is all bad because if everybody whined about everything, there would be no time left for the killing part, and we couldn't have that, could we?

Everywhere I traveled, from the DMZ to the delta, the entire country was pockmarked with the craters that were the only remaining indication of the deadly B-52 air strikes. I was amazed at how often I encountered them, from my first chopper ride to my last. They were everywhere: in the jungles, mountains, and the middle of the rice paddies. I'll bet that 99.99999 percent of them hit nothing but dirt—pay dirt, for the big fat cats back home that sold each and every bomb at a premium inflated price and then encouraged the liberal use of them. I was becoming a cynic about everything and everybody. Without even knowing it, I was getting mad. Slowly and surely the anger spread over my personality, poisoning every thought I had about anything, until I started to look to drugs for an escape.

More and more I found myself wanting to get high, until I was high all the time, and I wasn't the only one. The person I bought my dope from was the only black man who would talk to me socially—at least, I thought so, but maybe it was all business. Anyway, one morning I was going to his hooch to buy some grass and found him dead in his bunk, where he had drowned in his own vomit with a needle sticking out of his arm. Everyone I knew in Vietnam was high, either on drugs or alcohol—everyone. I don't think that anybody escaped the madness of Vietnam without some sort of mental damage. I know I didn't, and neither did my brother Mike. The whole thing was too much to bear and still keep thinking like you did before the experiences of war. Like I say, though, it happens so slowly that you don't notice it until, like your hearing, your mind is gone too.

Another thing I noted while flying around the country was that each and every road, firebase, or military compound, no matter how large or small, were surrounded by killing fields. At first I had the idea that someone must travel around and burn everything for a thousand feet around everything, but I eventually abandoned that idea because of the enormity of it. I mean, there was not a tree, a bush, or even a weed in most of the killing fields. I call them that because it was their intended purpose to give a clear field of fire for anything that didn't belong out there. I later heard the infamous words that I would grow to hate, along with the people who invented it, those who cashed in on the military sales and again encouraged its liberal use. The words were *defoliants* and *Agent Orange*. I know in my heart that the devil had a hand in the thinking behind such a thing as this, for it is purely evil. Its sole purpose is to kill anything that comes into contact with it, and it doesn't distinguish between plant and animal. It would kill everything that God created except the rocks and the dirt, but they were as good as dead because they were poisoned to the touch. They say that everything in life has its good side along with its bad, but I fail to see any good in this practice, unless I'm wrong and killing is good, but I'm pretty smart, and I don't think so.

The more and more I thought about it, I became convinced that Buddha was exacting his revenge upon my soul for shooting up his temple, because everything seemed to grow worse and worse. I began to feel that my whole life was centered on death and misery. Even the color of our uniforms began to symbolize something evil, and through contact with all these things that I considered to be based in evil, I began to feel I was a part of it. I could feel myself slipping into something that is beyond description. I recognized it eventually and realized that my father must have felt the same. He too had come into contact with evil, and he too had been whipped by it. He and I both had hoped to escape the feelings of fear and dread that go hand and hand with evil by going home. Not a chance! Things were just as bad at home. This I experienced firsthand when I went home on leave. People were rude, and they constantly pushed each other for more room, more money, more everything. The weak were trampled and ignored by most.

The only the ones that did change were those who felt they had lost it all and hit bottom. If they stayed alive, change was the one thing they could do; they couldn't stay at bottom or they would die, so they were forced to change. Those who felt they were losing their immortal souls and wanted to keep them were easy to spot. They're the ones that fed the poor, fought for the good in everything, and always wanted to try to make things right. They're the ones that have developed courage and strength. They don't carry guns, knives, or clubs. They aren't rude and they don't want to hurt you.

I'd say that a good 80 percent of Americans fall into this category. The other 20 percent are the ones that you have to watch out for. In Vietnam, of course, it's a whole different situation. You can't deal with that kind of evil; you just adjust to it. You adjust to it, or you die. It's that simple; you follow its lead or it will kill you or make you wish you were dead. I was beginning to notice something growing inside of me, and it was something new. I can't describe it exactly, but it felt like a dread or dismay, and my ideas of how I would live the rest of my life were changing. Everything that I had hoped would come to pass, every dream of the future had somehow disappeared, and it never came back. It was as if the simple, happy ideas and hopes that I ever had of happiness were just sucked out of my being.

I was a changed man. I would never be able to change back to what I was prior to Vietnam. I found that the old saying that you can never go home was true. I couldn't go home, but I could get high as hell, and I proceeded to do just that. I began to get high or drunk as often as possible, and the sad part of it is that nobody noticed the change in me because they were going through the same changes at the same time I was. The boys in Vietnam succeeded in doing one thing very, very well, and that was get totally fucked up. We were fine young men, fighting men. We were envied and feared throughout the entire world for the pride in our nation and the spirit in which we would defend her, but there was a sickness that was spreading among us. We couldn't see it, hear it, or feel it, but the people back home could sense that something was wrong with us, something just wasn't right with us when we came home, and they reacted by pushing us off. We, who went to Vietnam, gave so much and saw so much and lost so much. We were pushed off by those whom we loved the most. I found this to be true. It was the people whom I loved the most that hurt me the most. I was pushed off by the Paluskas. I can't describe how exactly because it was more of a feeling than something real, but it hurt. They were the ones that I held on to the hardest while I was in Vietnam. When everything else went to shit, I still had the Paluskas, or so I thought.

I found that during my second and third extension in-country, the mail came to a complete stop. I mean it stopped from everybody. Even with the fact that I wrote to them all, regularly, I don't think that I received two pieces of mail from home in my entire last year of service. In the end, I'm just glad that I wasn't married while I was over there because I'd hate to be pushed off by my wife, as happened to some of my friends.

I experienced several brushes with death in the following months and considered myself lucky to be alive. I began to live with the growing feeling that I would never make it home. I wanted to accompany a chopper that had been called on a Tac-E to Saigon that had to fly at night. I was told by the operations officer that I couldn't go because I was needed in Phu Hiep. This decision saved my life because the chopper crashed and burned, never to return. There was some duty that I had to perform the next day, and he wanted me to be fresh and well rested. I was well rested instead of dead. Another near miss with death occurred when a jet fighter appeared out of a cloud. It was so close that I didn't have time to tell the pilot it was there. We narrowly escaped a midair collision. I remember seeing the jet appear, heading directly for us, and I keyed my microphone to tell the pilot but could only make weird noises because I was so dumbfounded. I can remember the pilot saying, "Who the hell is this?" just as the jet flew past us, shaking the hell out of the chopper as it zoomed overhead. I was glad to find that as long as I still had some sort of fear, instead of indifference, at least way down deep—to find that I still wanted to live. But that feeling would soon pass also. I began to form a real I-don't-give-a-shit attitude, and it was mentioned several times by my superiors. But of course, I didn't care much about that either because I just didn't give a shit. My behavior became more erratic, to say the least.

While on guard duty, just before my second Christmas in-country, I really screwed up and nearly ended up in prison as a result. For some unknown reason, I was feeling really strange and weird. I didn't care much about anything. I still don't know why, but I walked from the guard post down to the wire that separated us from the nearby village. I took out a pin flare and shot it into the huge pile of straw on the other side of the wire and then watched as it went up in flames. I then drew my pistol and fired it, striking one of the oxen wandering around just on the other side. I shot it just to hear my bullet hit. I heard it hit the animal's buttocks with a thud. The ox did not fall, as I thought it would, but instead ran off toward the approaching Vietnamese farmers. They were visibly disturbed with me. I don't know what they were saying, but I do know that it wasn't nice. When they finally gave up and went away toward their huts, I thought that it would be funny to shoot at the feet of one of the old papasans. On the second shot, he went down, and then it dawned on me what I had done. I thought that I had killed him, but to my relief, he arose a short distance further away and ran for the huts. Just for good measure, I fired the grenade launcher into the middle of the rice paddy just to watch it explode.

I don't know what I was thinking, but it wasn't long before a jeep pulled up with two officers that wanted to know if we had been firing our weapons—which we denied, of course. We replied yes when asked whether or not we had a grenade launcher. With this they drove off to the next guard post. Chuck Straw, a blond surfer boy from California, ran his T-shirt through the M-79 to clean it, which probably saved my ass, because it wasn't too much later that we were relieved of guard duty and taken before the commander. If Chuck Straw hadn't cleaned the weapon and told me to keep my mouth shut, I would have confessed and been taken away to Long Bein Jail, and would have rotted inside one of those Conex containers out in the hot sun.

In the near future I would do other strange things, but none so dangerous to others. The lifers branded me as loony, and if I hadn't already applied and been accepted for my last extension, I'm sure that they would have sent me home. I was just a lucky fool. Shortly after our little incident on post number 13, Chuck Straw was killed in an aircraft accident. Chuck was there when I had first arrived in Vietnam. He was always making fun of "the lifers," as they were called. He finished his tour and went home, and I thought I would never see him again, but about a year later, there he was. During his time in the States, he had reenlisted and was then what he had hated the most about the army; he was a lifer.

My drug use got so bad that one night when the operations officer requested that I be called at night to find some maps for a mission to be flown the next morning, I was so high that I couldn't even find the maps they needed. I just went back to bed without finding them. I really caught it the next day, so I tried to straighten up for a while. It wasn't long before I returned to my old habits because I simply just didn't give a shit anymore. I was becoming very stupid in the manner in which I carried out my duties, and everybody noticed it. During a mortar attack by the VC one night, I climbed to the roof of our hooch so that I could watch the pretty explosions, and I tried to photograph the next attack with time exposures. I got some pretty good pictures, but they never made it home. I made tape recordings of one attack and sent it home to the Fredricksons, who were high-school friends of mine. I later learned that all it did was make them fear for my life, and I was told that they could not forgive me for that. They thought it was rude and cruel to send such a thing.

While in support of the 173rd Infantry Division, one of the sorties was to deliver a hot meal, kept hot in insulated, ten-gallon cans, and some large blocks of ice. I thought that it would be funny to take a bite out of each steak, and I proceeded to do so. By the time we got to the firebase, I had pretty well completed my mission, and then to top it off, when they carried the cans from the aircraft, I pushed the block of ice, sliding it down the ramp into the dirt. The block was covered with the red dirt, and I could see from their faces that they really wanted to give me special thanks for the extra dirt. I'll bet when they opened the cans and saw the steaks, they wanted to kill me. As a matter of fact, I could guarantee it.

Little stunts like that made life miserable for men who were already miserable. They were living in the worst of conditions on that fire base. Each man had a hole in the ground with a poncho for a roof. They were all unshaven and unkempt to the point that they reeked of sweat and grime. As bad as these men had it, the North Vietnamese had it ten times worse. The war had been going on continuously for a hundred years. For them it was commonplace to live on a single bowl of rice a day while living in holes in the ground. Serving in the military was for life or until they were dead or crippled so badly that they were sent home. They would have to walk home as best as they could. No trucks on the highway for them. No flights on passenger jets. They had to walk home just like they walked in, on trails cut through the jungle just wide enough for one man to pass another. For generation upon generation, Vietnamese children had never known their fathers. They were off fighting the current invaders of their homeland. Every male and some females served from early adulthood until death, and this surely is a life sentence of misery upon misery. To me a worthier enemy could not be found anywhere in the world. They surely had to be the finest soldiers in the world at that time.

Our invasions of Laos and Cambodia succeeded in pushing me so much closer to the brink of madness than I could handle. It was all I could do to keep my sanity and my wits about me. Most of the sorties that we flew were almost always the same. We would haul in fresh troops, ammo, and supplies while hauling out the wounded and dead. Over and over, day after day, and it was horrible for everyone involved—except for the munitions salesmen and the fat cats back home that were getting rich off this whole bloody mess. Death was everywhere, it stared into my heart, and you can never escape it in a war zone. Even though I tried to stop going along on the missions voluntarily, there were times when I had to get on an aircraft just to do my job. Even though I could not escape reality, I did manage to keep a dreamlike state, thanks to the local drug dealers, who seemed heaven sent to me. I really felt that it could not get any worse, but it did. Seeing the dead or the fear of getting killed or wounded was not the worst thing that you have to live with in a combat situation. I found that the worst thing that can happen to you, me personally, was killing another human being. The taking of another one's life kills you, on the inside, just as dead as the one you killed. I truly believe in my heart that everything that you do in this life, good and bad, will go around and around the universe and come right back to you. In your afterlife, I believe that you will have to make things right before you can find peace of any kind anywhere. I also believe that your existence will continue to be at a level of misery comparable to the act that you must amend to. Until the wrong is set right, it is the one thing that will haunt you and your soul for eternity.

It was a beautiful morning for a combat assault. A mist covered the ground that was so wet that you could stick out your tongue and get a drink. The white and fluffy sort of mist that will hide everything from view once you're above it. Up there it was bright, sunny, and cool. The cool air meant that we could carry a heavier load, and the clear air made us a better target. I say *us* because I needed a ride back to Phu Hiep. Since all three of our choppers were bound for the same destination, I was forced, out of necessity, to go along. If I wanted to get to Phu Hiep, this was my ride. The sun was just rising when our wheels left the ground. A sensation that I had grown to love slipped through my body with the help of some opiated weed that the gunner and I had just smoked. The Rolling Stones went from my helmet into one ear, out the other ear, and back into the helmet. I loved AFVN radio, especially while flying, low level, just above the treetops. For the first sortie, we had to pick up a sling load of thirty or forty hundred-pound bags of rice. My friend Rod asked me where we were headed, and I said, "To an ARVN fire base somewhere in the jungle highlands along the Ya Krong River. Near the Cambodian border somewhere," I yelled, so he could hear me above the whine of the turbine engines. COMO had sent us a message that a large force of NVA and VC were already staging an assault on a string of firebases that ran along the river. It turned out that our information was absolutely on target. The fire base was under enemy fire as we approached the tiny firebase, and the pilot was hoping to drop in quickly, set the load down, and get out again while the enemy was eating breakfast. It was not to be. As we were about to slip in and drop the load, VC started walking mortar rounds down the LZ toward us and the small-arms fire came at us from everywhere. The pilot punched the load while making a steep turn to escape the explosions. As I watched out the gunner's window, the sling load of rice hit the ground with enough force to break open all the bags and spread the rice practically over the whole firebase. The rice made it look as if the firebase was snow covered. In the short time it took us to circle and make a new approach, the ARVN artillery had silenced the enemy mortar fire, allowing us to drop off the few ARVN troops that we had on board, and we quickly loaded six or seven of their wounded and a few of the children that are so common around ARVN firebases. Women, children, and farm animals are the first clue as to weather a firebase is ARVN or not. Otherwise, they all look the same to me.

I can remember everything about this particular day just as if it were yesterday. The music that played through the helmet headphones at the moment of liftoff from the end of the first sortie was "Time Has Come Today," by the

Chamber Brothers. I can distinctly remember thinking that maybe my time would come today, just as time had come for the man lying on the ramp in front of me. I could see that he was bleeding to death, but I did nothing to help him. I don't know why, but I just looked at him, and I knew that he was as good as dead and that nothing that I could do would stop it. Then came the song "Lola," by the Kinks. *L-O-L-A*, Lola, L-L-L-L-Lola.

We returned on the second sortie with a sling load of artillery shells and small-arms ammo, in their long wooden boxes. It was easy for me to spot the white-capped hilltop, even from a long distance. I dreaded going back to that hellhole because we had been informed by some ARVN general named Cao Van Vien that his rangers of the 52nd Battalion were getting their asses kicked royally. We were told that he already had thirty dead and fifteen wounded, not counting the ones that were lying on the floor on our last sortie. In a matter of minutes, we had dropped the incoming load and hooked onto a VC 57-mm howitzer, and we were off. Boy, it was a beautiful-looking gun, too. Reinforcement troops were next in, with a load of their dead going out, and made up the following two sorties, and I knew that soon we would be hauling in a load of body bags because several of the ones now on our ramp held two bodies. I prayed that this was our last sortie, and I can remember how afraid I was becoming, and the whole firebase was hooded with a thick, black smoke that smelled like the shit burner's barrels. I did not want to go back again.

Of all the days to get stuck on a mission, I had to get stuck on this one. Buddha was surely mad at me, and I could almost make out his image in the smoke that swirled around the hilltop, and it scared the hell out of me. Just when I thought that it couldn't get any worse, a TAC-E was declared, and all sorties came to an immediate stop because one of our choppers was going down, and it wasn't a maintenance problem. They had been hit several times by small-arms fire while lifting off from their last sortie, and after trying to return home found that there was a bad vibration in their hydraulic system. A stream of white smoke flowed from the upper cowling, caused by the hot oil hitting the engine. It was all they could do to get down in one piece, with no time to pick and choose where to put down.

We could see the smoke in the distance as we sped as quickly as we could, hoping to extract the crew before the enemy engaged them. It only took minutes to get there, about the time that it took me to take out a cigarette, light it, and take one puff. That was all the time the VC needed to kill everyone aboard, strip their weapons, and mutilate their bodies.

Fear had grabbed me by the balls, and it shook me until I could not control my hands, shaking so violently that I could not drag the man who lay at my feet back to our chopper. I recognized the man's upper face as being a man from our company, but his lower face was gone. His upper teeth just hung there in open air, and all I could do was throw up. I tried to pull him by his Nomex shirt, but I could not grip it. My hands were like the claws on a lobster, stiff and unable to bend. As it turned out, I had to leave him there and run as fast as I could just to get back on the chopper that was powering up for liftoff and would have left me in a second if I hadn't gotten back in time.

The blades of the chopper were bent as far as they would go and popped louder than I had ever heard them before, in what I knew was a desperate attempt to escape enemy fire. I fumbled my way up to where the crew chief was firing and swinging his gun wildly, cursing as loud as he could. A round came up through the floor behind me and at almost the same instant another hit the crew chief's gun and deflected up through the roof. Enemy fire seemed to come from everywhere. As the chopper made a steep turn, I was looking almost directly at the ground, but I could not see a single VC anywhere. I was scared shitless. I realized that I had pissed all over myself, when I was almost knocked down from the rear.

It was Ronald Stiles, the gunner, who had stumbled and fallen backward and almost knocked me down too. For an instant I was angry, and I might have yelled at him, I don't know. It took a few seconds for me to realize that he was in trouble. He was opening and closing his mouth like a big carp, but nothing was coming out, not a sound. He sat there on his knees, with his feet up under him, opening and closing his mouth. I bent to see if I could hear what he was saying just as he coughed up blood all over me. For an instant I was angry again, until I realized that it was blood and he had not thrown up on me.

I remember forcing him to lie down, and he fought me for some reason. He was very afraid; I could see it in his eyes. I wanted to help him, but I didn't know what to do. I remembered that I was supposed to apply pressure to the wounds, but the blood was coming from his mouth, and I began to freak out because I didn't know what to do. A spot of blood grew on his shirt, so I pulled it open and found a small hole, almost in the center of his left upper chest. I remember how small and insignificant it looked, and as I wiped it off, it spat blood up into my face and then seemed to suck it back in. But for the coughing of blood, he seemed all right, and for a second, I thought it wasn't too bad. Then the coughing became so bad that I knew that he could not breathe, and every time he tried to take a breath, he would cough up blood.

I had seen a film about mouth-to-mouth resuscitation, and I found myself trying to force air into his lungs. My air was met with a torrid flow of thrown up Spaghetti-O's and blood, which forced me back to spit it out while throwing up myself. I remembered that his mother had sent him a care package that had contained the cans of Spaghetti-O's, and I had seen him eat some as we flew to our last sortie. I remember thinking all this and forcing myself to try again, which met with the same results. If we hadn't been so afraid, I know that we would have laughed at the whole thing.

He gripped my hand hard as I tried to hold the blood in his chest, and I could feel the strength drain from him. It was so quick. He tried to tell me something, but I couldn't make it out, and I shook my head as I looked down at him. His coughing stopped as suddenly as it had begun, and he returned to opening and closing his mouth like a fish. The look in his eyes changed from terrible fear to an empty stare off into space, and it took just a second before I knew that he was gone. I looked around, and I found that no one else had seen what happened. We were alone there, sitting on the ramp—all alone.

I tried to stand but was thrown toward the tail of the aircraft, which I found was spinning around at a terrible rate, and this brought a new level of fear that again gripped my ass and shook me even harder than before. The chopper was going sideways, and the blades were bent down almost below the windows. I realized that we were about to hit the ground, and we were going to hit hard. Around and around we went until the blades hit the ground, and with an awful roar, the ground came up right into the aircraft, right through the window. I could smell the grass, just as if I was using a lawnmower back at my mother's house. That was what crossed my mind as I got to my feet and looked toward the cockpit to find out what I was supposed to do. It was all I could do to keep my balance, and I found that the chopper was lying on its side, because I almost fell on the grass that stuck through the window at my feet.

I don't know if it was the pilot or the copilot, but one or the other stood in the doorway with blood on his face and screamed for me to run. I did not hesitate, and I thought that he was right behind me as I ran toward the rear of the chopper, out over the ramp, and into the tall elephant grass.

I was so afraid and I stumbled and stumbled as I ran. The grass was tall, over my head; it seemed to grab at me, scratching and pulling. It seemed to want to try to stop me. On and on I ran, and I did not look back for fear of the explosion that I knew was coming. I could smell the heavy odor of JP-4; the fuel that I knew was so flammable, so volatile. The only thing that I could hear was my own heavy breathing, and I was so afraid that I didn't even look for my crewmates. All I wanted to do was to get away from that chopper before it exploded. A thick black smoke surrounded me like a demon from hell, and I found it hard to breathe or even to see, but I kept moving on.

It was a raging fear, all consuming, as if it had a life of its own, and it took control of me as I was running for my life. I could feel the grass grabbing at me while the smoke filled my lungs and burned my eyes. The thick smoke seemed to fuel my fear because I couldn't see three feet in front of me through the wall of smoke and elephant grass. I could feel the heat singeing my hair, and I could hear the pieces of falling fragments that were all that remained of the chopper. Faster and faster I ran—until suddenly, there he was.

Everything stopped; it was totally quiet. I felt that everything was in constant movement around me but that time had slowed until everything stopped. I could feel the urine run down my leg again, and the memory of how Rod Sykes had wet himself as he lay there dying filled my mind in a flash. My wind was failing, and it was all I could do to breathe as I came face-to-face with a Vietnamese man.

He looked to be about fifty years old but was probably more like thirty-five. He was dressed in black, as most of the Vietnamese dressed in black silk pajamas. There was something in his hand that turned out to be a machete, and I somehow seemed to look at it and his eyes at the same time just as I'm sure he was looking at me. I could see that he had been cutting the tall grass and had made several piles that were tied with strips of cloth, probably for thatch to be used on his house. I could see that he was as surprised as I was at our meeting in the little room that he had cut with his machete. The walls of the elephant grass all around us, blocking the whole world from us just as if we were in a walled room. He looked away from me, as if he didn't want to see me and wanted to completely block me out. It was as if he didn't want the last thing that he would see on this earth to be me. It was as if he was looking for something else, or someone else. Maybe it was his wife or his children, I don't know, but I do know that he didn't want to look at me.

As I looked at him, he dropped to one knee and spun away and made a motion as if reaching for someone, someone who wasn't there, someone he would never see again, for I had ended all that for him. I had taken it away from him, and I didn't even know that I had. I had killed him, and I didn't even realize what I had done. It was already done before I realized that the pistol was in my hand. The spent shell was already lying on the ground, and the pistol was all ready to fire again before I knew that it had fired the first time. The bullet had already smashed into his chin and had flown out the back of his neck before he had even seen me. I didn't want to kill him. Now I could see that he was just a farmer that was out cutting thatch for some roof. Now he was half- sitting and half lying on the stubs of the cut grass, and he didn't want to see me, for I was the man who had killed him, and I was so stupid that I didn't even know that I had done it until it was already done.

I could not move, speak, or even breathe. It was coming to me, what I had done. I could feel it starting at my toes and coming rapidly toward the top of my head like a shock wave. What had I done? I could feel it grab my stomach, bending me over with pain, grabbing, clinching ever higher, until it struck my heart and squeezed it like it had some kind of bony fingers clutching at my heart and trying to tear it out. It was a mistake. I wanted to make it stop, but it just kept on coming and coming like something alive and evil. It was evil, and I had brought it to this world. It was born of my actions, and it would always be with me. I knew it the instant that it happened. What had I done? *What had I done?* I saw the brass lying on the ground, and I bent to pick it up. I held out my hand as if I were offering it to him. Jesus, Jesus, what did I do? Forgive me, please!

I was suddenly empty; I was wasted forever. I had done a thing that I knew I could never recover from. I was bound for hell and damnation for all eternity. I wanted to die. I wanted him to live. It was a mistake. What had I done? I was empty, empty of spirit, of happiness, empty of hope. I was empty of pride. I had done the unspeakable. I could feel my soul leave my body just as his was leaving his body. I remember hoping that my soul would go with his, entwine with his, and protect it from the evil that I had brought upon him. I hoped that it would forever be with his, for it was lost to me now, and I couldn't get it back. I hoped that both souls would go up with the smoke from the fire that nearly engulfed me, pushing me out and away from the man who lay there dead. I could still see the look that was on his face, and to this day the memory emerges at will, forcing me to relive that dreadful moment over and over—a memory to torment me for the rest of my miserable life.

I wandered through the grass aimlessly until I fell into a muddy trench and then crawled into the notch of an old burned-out tree, and there I passed out. It was almost dark when I awoke to the mumbled sound of voices, Vietnamese voices. I could smell their food cooking on the fire, lingering so heavy in the air that I could almost taste it. I yearned for the blackness that I had just awakened from, I wanted its peace and its quiet. I lifted my pistol to my face and tried to fire it, but it would not fire. It was completely jam-packed with mud, blocking its action. I prayed for the darkness to return, and it did, and I welcomed it with a new happiness. A happiness that hurt, and it always would hurt, and it hurts now as I fill these pages. I will always feel the cowardice, for I had run and left my crewmates to die. I had run without honor, without respect for myself or anything else. I had killed an innocent man, a farmer. He was not a soldier, of this I am sure, just a farmer that was in the wrong place at the wrong time, and I had cost him his life. How could I hide this true self from the eyes of others? Everyone would know!

I would never ask for forgiveness. I do not deserve it. It was I who would have to pay for this evil, and I knew it from the start. I had sinned, and for this there was no absolution, and I wanted none. It was my sin, and it was to be my punishment, my penance, for all eternity, never to ask for forgiveness, never, and I never have. That would be too easy, just as easy as it was to pull the trigger ending all love, life, and happiness for him and me at the same instant. We would be forever together, forever connected, through this life and into the next. From this moment on, everything would be easy for me, for I cared for nothing, one way or another. It's easy not to care, just as it's hard to care. If you want something, you have to care for it, yearn for it, and need it. I wanted nothing, I didn't even care if I lived or died, and I still don't.

It was there, while I lay in the mud, my mind coming and going, that I saw what I call an angel. She came to me as I found myself sitting in a large, intricately carved chair. She reached for me and grabbed my hand, leading me through a doorway to a balcony that overlooked a courtyard that was surrounded by a beautiful garden. There in the courtyard below were three men, whom I took to be servants, beating rugs with hooped wire whips. Each time the hoops struck the rugs, it made a popping noise. In an instant, I awoke on a stretcher, being loaded onto a chopper, a medevac chopper. In another instant, the darkness returned, and I welcomed it with open arms.

They tell me that for several weeks I was completely out of it, totally gone, out of this world. I was told that I was in the Mental Health Unit in Qui Nhon Hospital. For the life of me, I couldn't remember why I was there or what had happened to me. For a few blissful moments, I was free, but in a flash, it hit me. I saw the bloody face of Ronald Stiles, and then, the evil arose out of the darkness, casting me back into misery. For the first time in my life, I began to cry. I had wanted to cry many times, but I'd always been able to control it. Now, it controlled me. I could neither prevent it nor control it. I was overwhelmed by it. I was unable to stop crying for days on end; I could not sleep at night or function during the day. It was all powerful, and try as I may, I could not stop. I suppose it was very sad from the viewpoint of others, but they kept me there in the hospital until I got a handle on it.

My nurse, a round eye, as we called them, was named Judy. She was married to a naval officer that was stationed at Mare Island, California. Having told her husband about me and the deadly combat operation that I had been involved in, he found and sent a newspaper article that he had seen in his local paper. The article told of how three choppers were shot down and how there were seventeen US soldiers missing in action. I knew that they were all dead, and I'm sure that the commanders also knew, and it was beyond me why they wanted to hide it from the American public, but that's the way it was and probably the way it will be in the future too. During one session with the doctors, I was asked if, given the choice, would I want to go home to the States to finish my military service or would I wish to finish my tour here in Vietnam? My ETS (estimated time of separation) was less than five months away, so I asked for and received permission to return to my unit at Phu Hiep. It was there that I requested to be removed from flight status, never to fly another sortie over enemy soil. For the rest of my time in Vietnam, I was to work for the top sergeant. I never again set foot aboard a helicopter, and from that time on, I began to sink into a drug-ridden stupor. Lower and lower I sank, and it was obvious to all that I had a serious drug problem. It was by the grace of God that I completed my time in the army in an honorable fashion. I was lucky to have received an honorable discharge.

Over and over the subject of the "mission from hell," as it was called, was brought up by various members of my unit, and it almost always brought me to tears. I was like a waterfall, and everyone that cared about me did their best to console me. They all wanted to hear about what had happened to this person or that person, and it was all that I could do to keep control of my emotions, and soon they all seemed to catch on, because even the FNGs stopped asking. Someone at the hospital submitted my name for a decoration, which for some reason was pushed through, and sometime later I received a Bronze Star. I remembered that my mother had told me that my Father received the same medal, which made me think that perhaps we were not so different after all. We were two mentally ill soldiers with the same medal and the same addiction to drugs, so after all, we were pretty much alike in a lot of ways.

It wasn't two months before something else happened that was even worse than the shooting of the farmer. Four of us went to the armory and checked out a grenade launcher (an M-79) and an M-60 for weapons qualifications. In other words, we were bored and just wanted to shoot something up—anything, we didn't care. Off we went in a jeep to a field between our compound and that of the Korean White Horse Division. Soon we were all lined up and shooting at anything that moved. Birds, mice, or anything became a target. Behind us there was a large corrugated pipe, about five feet in diameter, and this too became our target. We must have put two hundred rounds into that pipe and several grenades.

Several of us walked to the pipe to look at the damage we had done when I heard a low moan from inside, so I ran to look into the end, and to my horror I saw a Vietnamese woman and two little girls covered with blood. I'm not going to give the names of the others that were with me that day, but the elder of our group went in to check on them and reported that they were all dead. I instantly began to throw up, and I don't think that I have ever felt lower or more evil than at that very moment. I would have killed myself right there, but my weapon was taken from me and I was practically carried back to the jeep which was promptly driven off by another of my friends. During the trip back I was told to keep my mouth shut and that this incident never happened. I was told that I was never to talk about it again because they weren't going to go to prison for those gooks. All I could do was nod my head in compliance. It would be more than thirty years before I would tell anyone about that day but it has always been there inside my head and it always will be. I have wanted to die almost every day since. This was the day that I lost my mind and soul.

My drug habit grew so far out of hand, that it's a wonder that I wasn't thrown out of the Army and put in jail, but thanks to the effects of these drugs, the remainder of my time in the Army flew by. I'm sure that if I wasn't so close to my ETS that some sort of disciplinary action would have taken place, and I would have lost my stripes at the least. The Top Sergeant had taken a liking to me and it was due to him that I was spared the humiliation of a court martial. It was he who handed me the BRONZE STAR, and His words still hang in my mind. He said that he was proud to have served with me, and of course, this brought me to tears, and I was truly afraid that everyone would think that I was a pussy, but for some reason, I was never accused of that. I'm afraid that not everyone felt that way about me, and as a result, I had but one enemy, Sgt. Carlson, was his name. I almost killed him with a tear gas grenade on the last night that I spent in Phu Heip. As he slept, I threw it into his hooch and locked the door, from the outside, forcing him to break down the door to get out. He was medivac'ed out of the country with burnt lungs, which to my evil delight, ended my last evening in Phu Heip. The next morning a formation was held to inform everyone that the grenade canister was to be fingerprinted, which I knew was bull shit, because the heat of the canister would destroy any fingerprints. "The person that threw it would be charged with attempted murder", they said. I snickered to myself for I was leaving that day and I was home free. Within an hour I was at the Air Force Base holding a flight pass in my hand.

It was about that time that I experienced what I now call depression, because it dawned on me that I was about to leave all my friends there, in enemy territory, again. I wished that I could take them home with me but I couldn't. I had to leave them, and it disturbed me more than I could have believed it would. As the big C-130 lifted off I had to fight back the tears, but they streamed down my cheeks anyway for I had lost whatever it was that I had as far as controlling my emotions. Whatever it was, it was gone, and the tears seemed to come and go whenever they wanted, and this would be the rule for the rest of my life. From that moment on I always found myself rushing into bathrooms or some quiet place to get a grip on myself, before everyone could see me. To my total amazement, I found that leaving Vietnam, the place that I hated so much, would be one of the hardest things that I would ever have to do. I guess what they say is true, life is stranger than fiction.

As soon as the C-130 landed at Bein Hoa Air Base I hopped onto a bus bound for headquarters and from there to register for transportation to the States for ETS. I found myself having to wait three days for my name to come up on the flight roster, which gave me plenty of time to think. As I did so, it became apparent to me that the good experiences, the good memories of Vietnam, were pushing their way to the forefront of my mind. I began to remember all the friends that I had made over the years, and soon I was grinning like an idiot, and it was because of that look on my face that someone asked me if I was OK. All that I could say was, "Oh yeah, I'm OK." I looked for and found the nearest EM Club, where I proceeded to get intoxicated for two days straight.

When I woke up on that next morning, I was burning when I urinated, a symptom that I knew oh-so-well as VD. I knew that, with a case of the clap, there was no way that they would let me go home. I guess they didn't want new strains of disease arriving and spreading over the continental US, which seemed understandable to me, but still I thought of not reporting it and trying to stand the pain until I got home. This proved to be a futile idea, for the next time that I urinated, it hurt like hell, and I went straight to the dispensary. They threatened to keep me in-country for the duration of the cure but instead gave me two painful shots of the cold penicillin and told me to stay away from the girls at home until it completely cleared up. This I promised to do, eager to get on that big jet airliner toward home. After being in the bar for two days, as you can guess, frequent painful trips to the urinal prevailed until my name came up on the transportation roster for 2300 hours that very night.

I reported at 2000 hours and waited and waited until they loaded us onto buses to be taken out to the middle of the runway where the big jet would touch down just long enough for us to board. As the bus left the terminal and headed out to the flight line, it suddenly came to a halt and was boarded by three MPs, one of which was an officer. He called for our attention by saying, "OK, listen up. We are going to search you for any paraphernalia. That is to include but is not limited to, weapons, drugs of any sort, body parts, or pictures of said body parts. At this time, we will exit the bus for a period of five minutes, which will give you all time to throw any contraband that you might have into a pile, right here on the floor where I am standing," he said. "At the end of those five minutes, a strip search will be conducted with the aid of search dogs, and anyone found to be holding contraband will be detained and you will never go home, so I suggest that you get rid of it now," he finished, and he left the bus. His foot had not left the last step when the stuff started flying. It didn't take long for the pile to grow enough for me to start going through it, and along with several others, ate whatever drugs were edible, and I ate something that I thought was speed but turned out to be a barbiturate. I didn't want to do it, but I feared being detained, so I threw out all my pictures of dead gooks. When I laid them onto the pile, I was amazed at how many pictures were already there, some looking just like the ones I had. I felt cleansed as I threw them out, and it was so easy to do. I have never missed them, and that period of my life I would love to forget, but it is impossible, for I will never forget. At that, the MPs picked it all up and sent us on our way without a search. Once on board the jet, the pills hit me and made me high and sick at the same time. I threw up several times and except for the painful trips to the urinal, I slept the entire flight.

The flight was over before I knew it, and suddenly I could see the lights of Seattle shining bright below us. There was a cheer of joy as the jet touched down on US soil, followed by a period of total silence, an eerie quiet that came when we all realized that we had survived. We had made it when so many others had not. Maybe we wanted to live more than they did, I don't know, I'll never know, but I had made it home. I kissed the ground at my first step on good old American soil, and it was grand, for it rose up to meet my lips like the lady she was, and I loved her more than I can ever describe, and I still do. Twelve hours later I was walking out the gate, and I gave a sigh of relief because the whole ordeal was behind me, and I would never have to think about it again—or so I thought. At any rate, that was the end of my army career, and I was glad that it was over.

Six

The very first thing I did upon arrival at the airport was go to the restroom and change from my military clothing into civvies, as we called them. I wasn't ashamed of them, but it was easier to deal with the American public if they didn't know that you were a soldier. At that time I did not know how I would react to the verbal abuse and the spitting from the hippie types. I was afraid that I would have to fight my way home if I wore my uniform, and I know for a fact that many returning Veterans suffered such abuse at the hands of the American public. My heart still breaks when I think of the way we were welcomed home. To this day I am so jealous of the way the current soldiers are welcomed home as heroes, while we were rejected and had to sneak home with our heads down. For many years I was so angry. I had no particular reason to be angry, but I was still angry, and I have never really gotten over it, and I probably never will.

My parents had retired and bought a small farm in Missouri, so that was my first stop, for I had applied and been accepted to attend Western Illinois University, and I had about a month to waste before classes started. On the day I arrived at my parents' house, I borrowed their car, went to the local Sears store, and bought a rifle. It was a small .22. To this day I don't know why I bought it, but I did. I took the rifle and went to explore the farm, looking for something to shoot. A small lake stood on the back of their property, and as I sat there watching the cattle drink, I could see the frogs jumping around, so I took aim and killed the first one. Over and over the frogs fell as I took aim and fired at every one that I could see. I don't know how long this went on, but before I knew it, there were dead frogs floating all over the lake. There were so many that the cattle would not even drink the water. Suddenly, it dawned on me what I had done. For the life of me I don't know why I did it, so I took the rifle back to the house and gave it to my little brother Dennis, and that was the last time I touched a gun for many years.

Although I had planned a lengthy visit with my parents, I found myself packing to leave the next morning, and I left that afternoon explaining that I needed some time to myself, which was true, because I found myself unable to relate to anyone in my family. The distance between us, I found, was further than anything I had expected, and I hoped at the time that it was because of my war experiences, but I was never able to bridge the gap that kept us apart. My brother Mike was living in East Peoria, so I headed that way in the hope of finding him, wanting to have at least some relationship, if possible. When the bus pulled away from my parents in Missouri, I remember distinctly thinking that my brother Dennis would surely be one of those people who would not make it home if he had to go to Vietnam. I had become quite proficient at picking those who would make it and those who would not, and I found myself doing it all the time, whether I wanted to or not. I figured that there were only two of the ten or so men on the bus that would have survived Vietnam.

Upon arrival in East Peoria, I had no idea where Mike was or how to find him, so I decided to call an old friend from school, Greg Adams. He seemed glad to see me, and the first thing out of his mouth was, "Did you kill anyone?" I heard this question over and over from just about everyone I talked to that knew I had been overseas. I always answered to the negative and usually changed the subject as quickly as possible. I spent the night with Greg and his family but moved on quickly the next morning. The next several nights I spent with Jill Fredrickson and her family, and I seemed to feel a little more comfortable there. Jill and I had always been very close friends, as she was as close as a sister to Penny Paluska. Jill's father thanked me for sending the elephant statues from overseas and showed me his entire collection every night that I was there, but the big teak-wood elephant that I had sent was his favorite, or so he claimed.

I finally found Mike on the third or fourth day, so I stayed with him until it was time to move into my dormitory at WIU. Mike and I hit it off well, and the fact that we were both Vietnam vets helped us relate to one another, even though we never discussed our experiences in Vietnam, good or bad. Mike, I found, was drinking a lot and using a lot of cocaine, but so was everyone else, it seemed, so I didn't think much of it. I had not used anything but alcohol since my arrival back in the United States, hoping that the drug abuse was all behind me, hoping to forget all about it and to lead a normal, clean life, but soon I found that all my peers were using one type of drug or another.

I arrived at school just a day or two before classes were to start, so I was one of the last to arrive on our floor (the eleventh floor) and therefore became the center of attention. Everyone wanted to know why the only thing I was moving in was a single suitcase. I didn't want to advertise the fact that I was fresh out of the army, so I simply told them that it was all I needed. As it turned out, it was lucky that I had nothing because my roommate had already filled our room with his things. This worked out fine for me because all I had was three changes of clothing, and they were all the wrong style for college. Talk about looking like a nerd—boy that was me, all right. My roommate, Tom Savage, turned out to be a really good friend to me, and without his help, I would have been a total outcast. I was totally out of touch when it came to the social scene and what was cool and what wasn't. He kept me in line, and he was one of the few people at WIU that ever knew that I had served in Vietnam. I accompanied him to his home in Chicago for Thanksgiving Day dinner, met his whole family and his fiancée, whom he had been engaged to for three years. Tom was a fine man, honest as the day is long, and as good a friend to me as I have ever had. The girls at school always seemed to chase him around, some coming right out and throwing a pass, but he was ever faithful to his girl at home. This amazed me to no end, because of all the men I have known through the years, I have only met one other that remained faithful to his woman, and that's a very, very sorry record indeed. I can remember that we often received obscene phone calls from women who wanted to talk to him in the middle of the night, and of course, often times I would act as if I was him when I answered. He didn't seem to mind, and of all the passes that were thrown at him, not once did he falter. What a character. He was unbelievable!

I wish that I could remember the names of my other close friends at WIU, but they have slipped my mind through the years. College was one hell of a party, and eventually the party got me kicked out of school. It took about a year and a half, but eventually I flunked out. That year and a half was one hell of a good time for me, and I truly needed the adjustment period to ease back into civilian life. Another sorry-but-true fact was that during this whole period of college life, I was celibate. I had not one sexual encounter the entire time, while everyone around me was really going at it, everyone except Tom. My entire sexual life, that is, everything I knew about sex, consisted of how to deal with Vietnamese whores. I had no idea at all how to go about having sex with a normal American woman, and even worse, I found myself unable to even talk with them except for the few friends that I made on my floor in the dorm. I was pretty much a loner, and that's pretty much how I liked it.

During this period I began to experiment more and more with drugs like LSD, mescaline, hashish, pot, and speed. Mike introduced me to cocaine, which of course, I fell in love with instantly. I couldn't get enough of it, and there was plenty around in those days. It became the drug of my choice until the first time I tried methamphetamine. I had tried different types of speed in the past, but nothing hooked me like this did. I will swear on a stack of bibles that meth is the most addictive drug that there is, with maybe the exception of heroin, which I was always afraid to try for fear of liking it too much, just like so many people I have known in the past. The people I watched slipped into some hell that I could see but that they seemed not to or didn't want to see. Anyway, as soon as I learned that someone was using heroin, I cut him or her off, and that was the last that I would see of them until they either stole something from me or overdosed. I was dead on the inside and I was judging others for their drug habits. What a hypocrite.

After flunking out of school, I moved in with Mike, where we proceeded to do every drug that we could get our hands on, except heroin, of course. Anything else was fair game. I began to eat LSD like candy, buying one hundred hits at a time until it took at least five doses of acid for me to get high. All I did for the next several years was get high. I didn't work or even look for work. Work would interfere with my party, and I sponged off everyone else to eat and party. I received not one complaint from anyone for at least two years, but eventually Mike grew tired of supporting my habits and threw me out of his apartment. By the time that this happened, I had been expecting it for some time and had arranged to move in with an old friend from high school and his wife. My brother and I ran in a very tightknit circle of friends that consisted of Mike and Vicky Hutchinson, Ken Steffen and several of his different wives, Pat and Shirley Hutt, and sometimes Bob Shelly and his sisters.

Ken Steffen was a Vietnam vet, so he was as screwed up as Mike and I from the beginning, but Mike Hutchinson had been in an automobile accident in which his brother Jack had been killed, so he was right up there with us when it came to getting messed up and high. Pat Hutt was probably the most stable of all of us, and he was probably the best friend that I ever had. He had a good job at the Caterpillar Tractor Company and never missed a day's work, even though we were partying like hell every night, usually until the early hours of the morning. It must have been hard for him to go to work, but he had a wife and daughter to support, and I have to say that Pat was a good man who always provided well for his family. Eventually everyone started screwing everyone else's wife, and it wasn't long before I was partaking of these pleasures.

Vicky Hutchinson and Shirley Hutt knew of my little (lack of sex) problem and were always pushing me to have a sexual encounter with them, joking at first, but it eventually became more and more persistent. It was easy for me to resist at first, for I had always considered myself to be a true friend, and I was for a very long time. They knew that I had not had sex for at least two years, and they really started to pour it on until I could resist no longer. It was Vicky at first and later Shirley, the wife of my best friend. It wasn't long until I was sneaking around and lying to all my friends so that I could be with their wives. I fooled them for a while, but eventually it all came out. Our little tightknit party group slowly began to fall apart, first Ken and his wife divorced, followed by Mike and Vicky Hutchinson, and finally Pat and Shirley Hutt.

Pat began to suspect that Shirley and I were having an affair and eventually started abusing her in a very physical manner. People would often see her with bruises and black eyes, and she never seemed to want to hide the fact, for she always told everyone what had happened. Pat was often seen beating her, and soon everyone was worried about her welfare, but all of this trouble did not slow our torrid affair in the least. We were together every time that he left for work, and it wasn't too long before they too separated. For obvious reasons, I sided with Shirley after the separation and Pat Hutt, my best friend, and I went our separate ways. Shirley and I went right on seeing each other, and soon everyone knew what was going on. Almost instantly, we became outcasts to all of our friends. They all came up with excuses why we should not come to their parties, and soon we were just about alone. My brother Mike and Ken Steffen were our only friends, and that's the way it went for the next year or so, until Shirley and I married, despite the fact that neither of us was in love with the other. It was almost as if we felt that we had to marry just to cover what we had done and to try to make everyone think that we were made for each other. The marriage was doomed from the beginning, and within a year, we were divorced. In the process, I had lost every friend that I had ever made in high school, and I had certainly lost any respect that I had ever had as a man and a human being. I am certain that this was the beginning of my heavy drinking days, and I was drunk for the entire next year. I will never forgive myself for my betrayal of my best friend, and I blame myself for the destruction of his family. I don't know whether it would have happened anyway, but it doesn't help the fact that it was an evil thing that I did to my friend Pat. I will always have to live with what I did. As bad as I feel about what I did, it would not be the last time that I would do such a thing, and the next time, it would nearly kill me.

I did not miss Shirley and was almost glad to be rid of her and all the things that she represented, so it was the very night that we separated that I began my next relationship. I went to my local hangout bar and ran into Beth Flannigan, whom I had dated while I was home on leave from Vietnam. She was a very beautiful woman, a divorcee that was several years younger than me. On that first night, we proceeded to get drunk and ended up in my brother's bed. From that night on, we were together for the next nine years. We married after several years of living together and were married for seven years. During the entire time that we were together, we were on a constant drunk. Even with the heavy drinking, we seemed to function fairly well because we both held good jobs. We eventually moved to California, where she went to work for I-Magnum and I went to work for Kiewit/Pacific Construction, where I built bridges and high-rise buildings all over the state. We did well financially and soon owned a nice home in the Berkeley Hills above the Claremont Hotel, which was a very nice area but was completely destroyed by a firestorm in the late eighties. The drugs took me, and the booze took Beth, and that was soon the end of our marriage. Beth asked me to move out of our home one night. I respected her wishes, and that was the last I ever saw of her. I missed her for a long, long time and considered the divorce to be mainly my fault.

By this time I had been in California for five or six years, and Mike had joined me and married a lady named Anna Aluno. Anna and I hit it off from the first time that we met, and I felt that she was a good influence on my brother and would keep him out of trouble. Shortly after my divorce from Beth, I moved in with them in their small house in San Jose. Anna's father, Ed, offered to remodel a shed behind Mike's house if I would help with the work and pay rent for some time afterward, which was just what I needed, so I agreed. Ed Aluno was one of the finest men whom I have ever had the privilege to know. He was badly wounded by German artillery during WW II, and his bent and broken body went from here to there and everywhere without a whimper or a complaint. We grew quite close as we worked on that old shed, and I got to know him very well. He was a man ahead of his time, and he had an uncanny sense of future events and what was to come to be. He had the sense to buy up as many of the old dilapidated houses, at near nothing, all around the down-town San Jose area. Some of the old houses, with no foundations and falling apart, sold for millions of dollars upon the downtown renewal projects that have made San Jose so beautiful today. He did not live long enough to see them sell for so much, but his widow, Jo, is now a very wealthy woman. Ed's death was very hard on me, and I'll never forgive myself for not going to see him at the hospital to say good-bye. Ed was a good friend to my brother and me.

My separation from Beth had broken my heart, but it wasn't hard for me to put her out of my mind, for I had trained myself all my life that if someone is gone, they're gone for good, so move on and forget them as soon as possible. It had always been easy for me to do, and I always warned anyone that I had any sort of relationship with that they should never tell me to leave because I would, in a second, never looking back. This had been easy for me too because as far as I was concerned, they were one in the same. Staying and waiting to leave was just as bad as leaving. It was always clear to me that no relationship, no matter how close, would always be just a few feet from ending. I was always ready for either them to leave or for me to leave, it didn't matter to me. I always knew that it was just around the corner and that nothing was permanent. No relationship would last more than a few years. That's the way it always had been, and that's the way it always would be. I had accepted that fact many years ago, so I was not looking for anything or anyone to be around for long. The only thing was that I was lonely, and I missed having some sort of romantic relationship, so I went to my sister-in-law for help.

I asked Anna to set up a date with one of her friends for me, but she wouldn't do it because she said that she had already picked someone for me that she knew I would like. That evening we went to dinner, and afterward we went to the house of a girl named Therese Silva. She was a divorced mother of two, beautiful in her own way. She had a crooked sort of smile that seemed to draw me toward her mouth. Her children and I hit it off from the start. She had a son, Ricky, who was four years old, and a daughter, Jennifer, who was three. Ricky was very protective of his mother, and every time that I got too near her, he would work his way between us. I admired the boy and thought that he and his sister were just wonderful as far as kids went. I had no experience at all with children, and I really wasn't looking to have a relationship with a woman with kids. Just a short visit was all we had that first night, but I knew that I would see her again because she was just the kind of girl I was looking for. Within two days I was on the phone asking her for a date but was promptly turned down. I didn't give up and called her several more times, but the answer was always the same: no thanks. After several attempts I gave up and told Anna that if she wanted to ever go out with me, she'd have to ask me now. I thought that was the end of it, and I'd never hear from her again. I just figured that I wasn't her type.

It wasn't two days later that she did call, and we agreed to meet at a park where the kids could run and play while we got to know each other. Therese was different from any other girl I had been involved with; I don't know how exactly, but very different. She was very thin, with very small breasts, and she was definitely not my usual style. Another thing that I noticed that was different was that she was "low maintenance," and I was used to women who were always wanting this or needing that or always buying something to wear, and if not that, then they were shopping for something to buy. Therese didn't seem interested in all that, and that was one thing that I liked about her from the start. I thought that it must be an act, but Anna assured me that she was everything that she seemed to be. I was definitely interested in having some kind of relationship with her but was a little hesitant because it seemed a little too easy to like her.

I was already seeing another girl named Joey, and she fell into the category that was the same as all the other women I had relationships with in the past in that she was very high maintenance, big busted, and very beautiful. She owned her own home with a swimming pool, and had a very good job at Atari Computers. Joey was a lovely girl, and I liked her very much, but when it came to choosing between her and Therese, there was no hesitation at all, I and never regretted choosing Therese. Joey was very possessive and was aware that I was seeing someone else, as did Therese. Both wanted me to stop seeing the other, but it was Therese that I thought really needed me. It wasn't that she couldn't get along without me, but she made me feel that she needed me. Joey wanted me to move into her house with her, but I never felt that tingling feeling that I felt with Therese, and that was what made the difference. That is why I wanted to stay with Therese, and I have never regretted it.

It wasn't long before Therese and I moved in together, and it didn't take her long to figure out that I had a drug problem. She never cared much for drugs, which was lucky for me because, as it turned out, she is the only person in the world that could keep me from going crazy. My drug habit kept growing and growing while any desire, on her part, to use any kind of drug just seemed to die out. At first she didn't complain about my increasing drug use, and for many years, she put up with me and all the dirty little habits and changes in my personality. I cannot tell you of all the hell that I put her through; it would take a million pages. It was like I had her totally under my control, and I would use the fact that she loved me to my advantage to get what I wanted or to do what I wanted. The sorry thing is that all this time I knew what it was doing to her, how it was hurting her, and it didn't seem to bother me at all. Getting high was all important, and I didn't much care what I had to do to stay high. I wasn't picky; I would lie, cheat, and steal from anyone to get what I needed. If Therese ever thought about leaving me, she never mentioned it to me, and the thought never crossed my mind that she was unhappy with the way things were going.

To this day, it still amazes me when I think of the power of her love. Therese is so strong, not just in her love life but in everything she does, except for one thing. It is beyond her to understand why other people think and say that she is pretty or, as I believe, beautiful. She has the impression, and I don't know what or who put it there, that she is plain or too skinny or too fat. I never thought her anything but beautiful, and she is constantly telling me that she thinks that I don't like this or that about her, which is anything but true because I fell in love with her the very first time that I set eyes on her.

As long as I had my drugs, I could function pretty well at work, and things went along in an almost normal manner. When I did work, I usually did well and had no problem getting promotions and raises. The problems arose, always, when I ran out of drugs. I found it increasingly harder to even get to work, and harder still to function when I got there. It became necessary to spend more and more of my paycheck to satisfy my needs, until I was spending half of it on dope. Therese seemed to be satisfied with anything that I gave her, or at least, she kept it to herself if she didn't. If she needed extra money, she always tried to let me know at the beginning of the week, before I had spent too much. This worked for a while, but soon it got to the point where Therese had to go to work herself, and as I think back, she must have worked most of the time to make ends meet.

I cannot say enough about Therese, and I have no words that could correctly describe her personality to you. Those of you that have had the privilege to know her understand what a challenge it is to say what a good person she really is. Her character is so strong, and it seems to get stronger with each passing day. I can only believe that this strength of character is genetic in nature, for her sisters seem to have the same strengths. Therese has always been so much stronger than me, and I've always known it, but I've never resented this fact for even a second. Oh, I might have rebelled a few times when she got between me and my drugs, but I've always known instinctively that she was always basically right in anything we've ever argued about. I truly don't know if she has ever lied to me about anything, which is amazing to me because I was constantly lying to her, about just about everything. I would lie about the stupidest things, and it made no sense at all, but she never let on unless she was angry with me, and then I would lie to get out of my last lie. She must have thought that it was never ending! I'll never know how someone like her could love someone like me for so long and put up with such obvious lies, neglect, and mistreatment. I guess that's the difference between her and me, because if the roles were reversed, I could not have put up with it. I would have split with the wind.

Therese has been a blessing, a gift from God given to me for some reason known only to God. God has chosen me to be the man for Therese. When I say or think about what has been given to me, a wonderful warm feeling comes over me, and for some reason I have come to believe that I actually deserve her. Obviously, God must have thought so, too—don't you agree? For many years I was afraid that God had given her to me simply to punish me by taking her away. I was always prepared to lose her, it seems, but I've become a lot smarter lately because I know now that I will always have her in my heart. Each and every beat of it will whisper her name to me until that day comes when God decides it's time that we will be together for eternity, and when I see her standing next to God, I will know her true spirit and her true soul. I know in my heart that it will be a beautiful moment, and for this reason alone, I no longer fear death as I once feared life. When death takes me to where ever it takes me, I will wait only for her, and when she comes, we will be happy forever.

I know now that the cloud that surrounds your soul when you are high on drugs obstructs your vision, and you sometimes see things that aren't there, and you sometimes fail to see things that are. Things are twisted and turned by something other than God. Things are hidden and changed at its will, as it has a life of its own. To become a good addict, you must surrender yourself wholeheartedly, or it just won't work. I can tell you that I was totally under its control, and I can also tell you that if it happens to you, you will not like it. I hated it, for it constantly broke my heart, tore me apart, and put me back together just as it wanted to and made me into another person, and I hated him too. I can only compare it to sitting in a seat in a theater, watching your life being shown on the screen. On drugs, I could sit and watch my life go by, but like the movies, I had no control over it or what happened. I did neither wrote the movie nor could change anything about it, even though many times I tried desperately to stop it or turn it off, but I could do nothing. This thing, this force that takes you over and tells you what to do, will never go away once it has you. I tried everything. I tried to stop on my own, I went to a rehab house, and I went to God. Nothing could send it away, and God seemed to ignore me, so I began to think of my old friend, death.

I was thinking of death when God gave me something to live for: a son. Therese told me that she was pregnant, and my reply to her was, "Well, I can't kill it, so I'll leave the decision up to you." I remember saying this, and it wasn't that I didn't want a child, it's that it never dawned on me that someone would even consider going through all the pain and trouble to have a child with me. The way I was thinking was that Therese needed money to take care of it, to do away with the child. This is how sick I really was. I just assumed that Therese would never have a child with me, so I had always thought that I would be childless and that I would die alone in some alley. It took a while, but it finally dawned on me that Therese was going to give me a child, and that she did this of her own free will. She wanted a child with me.

The very next day, I bought two golden rings, took them home, and asked her to marry me. Within a week or so, we eloped to Reno, Nevada, and we were wed. Of course, I was high at the time, and much of our marriage has escaped me over the years. I was high for the duration of the pregnancy, and I was high when my son was born. The only thing that I can remember about the whole birth was the pain on Therese's face and the feeling of joy when I first set eyes on my son. I was still in the theater, watching my life on the screen, with no control, as usual, but there was one thing different about this scene. This scene in my life was written by Therese, my wife, my love. Therese was in control; I could see it clearly now. It was from that moment, I think, that I surrendered. I knew that she knew what to do, and all I had to do was to let her do it and it would be as she wished. I wanted her to take control. I hoped that she would take control, and she did, but she could do nothing to stop my drug use, try as she may.

It wasn't long until the police got wind of my drug use and I was arrested, put in jail, and expected Therese to come up with the money to get me out, and she did. I had been arrested for the possession of a controlled substance, a felony that was kicked down to a misdemeanor upon completion of probation. A second felony arrest followed quickly when I sold thirty dollars' worth of drugs to an undercover narcotics officer and was arrested for sale of a controlled substance. Before I could complete the probation for these arrests, I was arrested four or five more times. The last of which was the straw that broke the camel's back, as they say. I had finally made the big time, as I was bound to go up the river, so to speak.

I was locked up away from Therese and the kids, and it's pretty much where I belonged. Everything was all screwed up. I was out of control. When I say I was out of control, I mean out of control. I was truly a mess. I had been committed into a mental hospital not once but twice. I had taken up the habit of beating myself with a stick, almost daily, sometimes until it bled and scarred. I had injured myself when a booby trap I was building (to get even with some asshole) went off on me instead, tearing a gaping hole in my arm, an injury complicated by the fact that I was too stupid to go to a doctor for several days until it became infected.

My life was a mess, and I felt that I was ruining any chance that Therese had for happiness. I was doing a fine job of that. In the past few years, before my last arrest, I had cheated and been caught by Therese having an affair with a bag whore (as they say). I was mad at the world, I hated everybody except for Therese and the kids, and I felt that they were better off without me, so I mistreated them terribly.

I was going to go to prison and I truly deserved it, even if I did think at the time that "they were out to get me for no reason." Yes, I was back in my theater, watching my life movie, and this time Therese could not help me because she had not written the scene. Therese again spent money that we didn't have to get me out of jail for a few precious days so that I could say a proper good-bye before going up the river, but four days later, I was back in jail, and I knew that it would be a long time before I was released. As I sat in jail with plenty of time to think and no drugs readily available, the real world slowly showed itself to me, and I didn't like it. I don't think that I could ever remember what it was like in the real world. I was into my early fifties, and I had been high since my early twenties. As long as I can remember, someone who either abused me or mistreated me had controlled my life, or the drugs that I was using controlled it. It's as if I had been sitting in that theater, watching my life on that screen, with no control over it for thirty years—thirty years! The big three-oh. Boy, what a waste. My whole adult life was a total waste of time except for the few moments when my son, Joey, popped out, all bloody, squealing like a pig. That was the best moment of my life to that point in time. As I sat there thinking, I slowly realized what I had really done to my dear wife, Therese. I had torn her heart out and stomped on it many, many times, and now I was doing it again, and this time I thought was the last chance she would give me, and that when I was shipped out to prison, she would meet and fall in love with someone else, someone who would treat her right, as she should be treated. Yes, I felt that I deserved to go to prison, but I sure was not looking forward to it.

Seven

Two years and eight months was my sentence. Of this time, I could expect to serve at least sixteen months, with time off for good behavior. I received credit for four months that I served in county jail, so that knocked it down to a year, or so I hoped. I had it all figured out before I was loaded onto the bus for the trip from Yolo County Jail to the California State Prison at Tracy. The bus was packed with all types of tough-looking characters, only one of which I was aquainted with. He had been in the same dormitory that I lived in at county, and he was well educated on the dos and don'ts of the penal system. John was a crankster gangster from Sacramento, short and heavy, and he walked with a limp because of a softball-sized open wound on his upper left thigh. The story that he gave me about the wound was that he had developed a sore on his thigh when he would shoot up heroine over and over in the same spot until he developed an infection that was so bad that it began to eat the infected flesh. Having seen the open wound, I can tell you that I've never seen anything like it, and I thought I'd seen it all. Anyway, John eased my mind about what was to happen when we arrived at state prison, for I had been having all sorts of scary visions in my mind about what would happen. In the end he made my first couple of days in prison so much easier for me, and if I ever see him again, I'll buy him a six pack of beer.

We were chained from head to toe for the bus ride to Tracy, which made the two-hour trip almost unbearably uncomfortable. It was impossible to sit comfortably when your hands are cuffed behind you in a bus so crowded that I could count the hairs in John's nose. With all of this, add the fact that I tried to give John a little extra room for his hurting leg, and he whined the whole trip.

I would like to say that this was the worst day I had in prison, but it wasn't. After what seemed like an eternity, the bus pulled off the freeway, and I got my first glimpse of the state prison at Tracy, California—first, the guard towers, then the housing units. It was surrounded by such horrific-looking fences that no one but a Viet Cong would try to cross it. The big fence opened up its mouth, and in we went. I have to admit that it was a little like my arrival in Vietnam, guns and all, and this opened my mind to all sorts of memories that had long ago buried themselves deep in my subconscious, where I thought they would remain forever.

In Vietnam, I felt tough, and I believed that I was tough enough to survive, and now I was tough again. I must be tough. Everyone was tough, from the inmates to the guards, and even the civilian workers looked tough. Nerves and tempers were on the razor's edge, and one wrong word or look and you would be beat down with no mercy, none at all. The best that you can hope for in prison is that no one, I mean, no one, notices you. Blend in, stay quiet, obey the rules, and maybe you'll get through the first day in relatively good condition. Therese was all that I could think of as I was told to strip off all my clothes and bend over for some gorilla of a guard to look up my ass before being herded into the smallest room that they could find to leave us all in our shame in for the next hour, while the guards passed by as if trolling for queers. Naked, we filled out endless forms, saw a medical clerk, ate bologna sandwiches, and then waited some more until we were finally given orange jump suits, none of which fit anyone. Finally I received an interview with an ugly-looking sergeant that asked me if I was a queer or if I had any enemies that I knew of before herding me off to another holding cell for another two hours. Next it was pictures, fingerprints, and an information book about the rules and other pertinent information concerning life in lockdown.

Around noon, we were herded out into a grassy area and told to wait until we were called and assigned to a cellblock. It took all of ten minutes before all hell broke loose, and the sirens were blowing and the guards were screaming and next came the pop, pop, pop, of the block guns. In another instant, fifteen guards appeared out of nowhere and proceeded to surround and beat down anyone that wasn't lying face down in the dirt. The similarities just kept coming and coming, and soon I could feel myself slipping right back to Vietnam, just as if I had never left. Over and over certain things would be said or happen to take me back, back where I dreaded going. It was at that instant that I knew that I was on my own again, and I'd better pick up my head and quit feeling sorry for myself and pay attention to my new environment, keep alert at all times, and always be aware of what was happening around me. There was a whole new set of rules here, and I'd better learn them quick because trouble was all around, searching for someone, and I didn't want it to find me. It must not find me.

The whole place seemed like something out of the nineteenth century to me, with its towers, fences, and cops with clubs, treating the inmates like they were pieces of dirt instead of humans. The further I got into the dungeons, the further back in time I seemed to go, and except for the automatically closing cell doors and the electric lights, it really *was* the nineteenth century. At long last I was assigned to a cell, which happened to be on the third tier, in the middle of a row of about fifty cells. My new cell mate happened to be from the city of Davis, so we had a lot to talk about at first, like how small the cell was and how long we could expect to be held in reception before being sent out into the penal system, hopefully to a fire camp where the living was supposed to be more bearable. We found that there was nothing, nothing at all, to do in this cell except talk and sleep, but a person can only sleep so long before he's wide awake, and then that is where the problems start. In a cell as small as ours, five feet by six feet, with two bunks and a toilet, it isn't long before you and your cell mate start bumping into each other.

At first, everything is fine, lots to talk about, getting to know each other, but soon you learn to hate each other and each other's nasty habits. You hate his odor, the way he talks, the things he says, and eventually even the way he looks. It isn't long after that one or the other of you is going to get knocked out. Fortunately, I've always been lucky when it comes to fist fighting, not that I'm an expert or anything like that, but experience counts for 80 percent of any fight. I'm a true believer in that. The real problem that goes hand in hand with lockdown fighting is the scary fact that there is no one, no third party, to stop the fight if it goes too far. If a person loses his temper or doesn't have sense enough to control himself in these situations, someone will end up dead, and then you have another serious charge, adding more time to what you already have. Nevertheless, lockdown fighting was quite common in reception at Tracy.

Evening in prison is the strangest thing that I think I have ever encountered. There is no quiet, no peace, because the rappers are rapping, the singers are singing, the poets are telling poems, and the madmen are raving, all at the top of their voices, out the windows. I found myself screaming right along with them, and I guess I would put myself into the madman category because I can't rap or sing, and I sure ain't no poet. Every night this would go on until I could finally get to sleep, hopefully to dream of home and about Therese, my sweet Therese.

It had been years since the last time that I said a prayer, but on the first night at Tracy, I began to pray for God to protect my family and to watch over them until I saw them again. It was a habit that I held true to every night. A person can drive himself insane worrying about things at home while he's locked up, and it takes real fortitude to force yourself not to do it. Naturally, you will worry, and I did.

I worried that Therese would find a new man and that someday soon I would receive divorce papers in the mail. I worried that my son, Joey, might need me and that I wouldn't be there for him. Many, many nights I lay awake and worried myself into a frenzy, knowing all the while that I had absolutely no control over what happened on the outside. It took many months to get control of myself in this respect, and I often slipped back, having to get a new grip on myself again.

The state prison at Tracy is a huge prison, housing every type of criminal that you could think of, and in reception, they are all housed together. The hardened criminals are placed right along with the petty thief or drug offenders. Men who have a lot of time facing them care little of the feelings of a man who only has six months, and sometimes they will go out of their way to give him more time by starting fights or by just simply taking his belongings. If a hard timer wants something, he will usually just take it, and if you object, a fight ensues—and, therefore, more time and another charge. A vicious circle, indeed. In prison, if you're not tough enough to keep your belongings, well, they're gone, and there's nothing you can do about it except join a prison gang for protection. In prison, you have no friends; you have what they call dogs. Dogs can be good or bad. Sometimes your dogs will turn on you and you will find yourself in the hospital or in the hole.

I learned quickly who I could associate with and who I couldn't. At certain times it is permitted to talk to just about anyone, but on the yard, it's a different story. As you walk around the yard, you find that certain areas are controlled by different groups, some of whom will attack you for even a wrong glance or for sometimes hearing something that you that made them think you were insulting them. Just about anything under the sun could spark it off on the yard, and it was a daily affair. Riots and fights are regular occurrences in prison yards, and they sometimes escalate into brutal gang beatings, where fifteen men attack one individual for this reason or that. All you can do is pay attention to what's going on around you and know who is who and who to avoid.

Gang members were everywhere: the blacks, the Muslims, the Indians, the northern Mexicans, the southern Mexicans, the Chicano Mexicans, the Asians, the whites, the Inland Empire, and the he-shes who looked and smelled more female than male. In riots, the whites and the southerners were against the blacks and the northerners, but usually the big riots were between the northern and the southern Mexicans. For some reason, some imaginary line that divided northern California from southern California was a hate line, and it became a line that sent many Mexicans to the hospital, to the hole, or even to their death. The northern Mexicans were under lockdown the entire time that I was in prison, coming out for meals only, which I'm sure made life in their cells a holy hell. If the fighting escalated to a certain point, the entire prison would be locked down, and meals would be brought to the cells, and no one except kitchen workers got out. Each gang elected a representative who could hopefully settle disputes before it got to that point, but not always. There were instances where a certain gang member would insult another gang, and to stop a riot, each gang would handle its own people, sometimes assaulting its own member to satiate another gang. It is good policy to stay out of another gang's affairs, and it's one that I adhered to avidly.

I don't know how it happened, but I ended up hanging with the Inland Empire guys, not only for protection, but for the social life. On the yard, if you're alone, you're easy pickin's. The Inland Empire guys just seemed to adopt me, and I was grateful for everything that they did for me.

It was two long weeks before I was moved to a new cell with a new cell mate. The new cell mate was a real criminal-type guy on his tenth violation. He had been locked up for most of the last ten years and was facing another year. He was from the city of Lodi and had caught a manufacturing charge and a whole lot of violations. I told him that he should move away from Lodi, but moving is impossible as long as you're on parole. On parole, you live exactly where they tell you to. Another two weeks passed slowly, but I learned a lot from my new cellie, like how to make a blowgun to blow a string from cell to cell in order to transfer and trade just about anything under the sun. It wasn't long before we were rich in postage stamps, which we used as money. Stamps could buy anything—cigarettes, drugs, or even sex. Whatever you wanted, you could get for stamps.

It was four long weeks before I was taken to see a counselor, who told me that I was qualified to go to fire camp if I so wished. I certainly did. Within three days, I was shipped to Sierra Conservation Camp at Jamestown, where I was to train as a wild lands firefighter. I was chained up and loaded onto a state-transport bus, which was manned by the toughest sons of bitches I have ever run across in my life. I mean, they were tough; these guards would beat you for sneezing too loud. The bus ride from Tracy to Jamestown was taken in total silence, not a peep from anyone. I don't care how tough an inmate was; he did not mess with these guards at all.

Jamestown was not what I expected. For some reason, I had thought it wouldn't be a prison, but that's exactly what it was, and a mean one, too. I was lucky enough to be sent to the two yard, where the violence is at a minimum. Even so, fights were a daily routine on the yard.

I received my first visit from Therese at Jamestown, and I was so happy to see her. Therese was there to visit at the earliest opportunity, and it was a joyful moment when I received the notice to go to the visiting center.

The doors to the yard were opened only once an hour, so I had to wait patiently for half an hour before I could journey toward the gate that led to visiting. Once at the gate, I was forced to wait until a notice from the visiting officer to the officer at the gate before my ID was checked, and then I would be allowed through the gate for my visit. Finally my name was called, but I was told that I could not pass through the gate without a T-shirt, which I had neglected to put on, and therefore I would have to wait until the next unlock, go into the dorm, get a shirt, wait for the next unlock, and then start all over while Therese waited in the visiting room. On my way back to the dorm, I asked a stranger on the yard if I could borrow his T-shirt, and to my surprise, he complied, so within one half hour, I was in Therese's arms.

We were allowed a short kiss and a hug before and after the visit, which was observed closely by guards and cameras placed all around. She was so beautiful, and my prayers were answered because she still loved me after all that I had done to screw up our lives. I am so thankful for her love. She assured me that Joey would come for the next visit, and that really gave me something to look forward to. I had been in prison for only five and a half weeks, and it already seemed like an eternity.

It takes something like that for some people to realize what they have to lose, and I'm just unlucky enough to be one of them. It took being away from Therese for me to really see how much she meant to me. I'm sure that if not for the love of my wife, I would still be locked up for some unspeakable crime.

At the conclusion of the visit, I was stripped searched and returned to the yard. Leaving Therese in that room was terribly hard to do, and only her promises of another visit as soon as possible reassured me of some future happiness. Once back on the yard, I was free to roam around the track and stop and chat with the few inmates who I cared to associate with. The yard was the major source of information—mostly incorrect, but if you could gather information from enough sources, certain information could be confirmed, such as the length of time it would take me to be assigned to a training class for my physical fitness course. This course had to be successfully completed before I could be assigned to the firefighter-training course. From the information that I could gather, the whole thing from beginning to end would take about six months.

It was three months later that I was finally assigned to a Physical Firefighter Training PFT class, and of course I waited until the last possible moment to start getting into some kind of physical condition. During my wait for PFT, I did the minimum amount of exercise that was allowed, for I was told by the white representative that it was required of all whites to be in some sort of condition and always be ready to come to the aid of any white inmate that was in trouble. Refusal to aid another inmate of the same color was dealt with harshly by the rep and his goons. On the other hand, one physical altercation could keep you from training and fire camp.

Once in PFT, the training began hard and got tougher each day. Five days a week, four hours a day of the toughest workouts that I'd had since basic training in the army. Still, this training was similar but much easier and with less discipline. I was right on the borderline because of my age, which was fifty-two. I think the average age of the inmates at fire camp was probably around thirty or thirty-five. I successfully completed PFT, but at the finish, I could barely walk because my legs were so sore. I had to walk what was known as the Jamestown shuffle, which was a sort of waddle due to the soreness in the upper thighs. I would begin a job in the kitchen and await assignment to a class in firefighter training (FFT).

Two months later I was in FFT. This training I really enjoyed and looked forward to, for it meant assignment to a fire camp, which was the best that you could expect in the state prison system. Camp was the Cadillac of the penal system, the best food, the best treatment, and the best pay that you could expect from the state. The pay, while fighting a fire, was one dollar an hour, and boy, it was surely welcomed. I just seemed to whiz through the training, and before I knew it, I was on my way to the fire camp at Owen's Valley, which was in the high desert near Bishop, California. Everything I had heard about fire camp was true. Life was good; as good as it could get being in prison. Even with the daily job assignments, which consisted of cleanup and weeding of local roads and the county fairgrounds, life was good. There were daily excursions out into the public, riding in the back of a big red fire truck, and all the kids would wave at us, greeting us just as if we were free firefighters. At first the fires were small grass fires around the Bishop area, but with the coming of fire season, soon we were sent to the larger, meaner fires that were considerably more dangerous. Danger and all, I loved it. I loved the excitement and the danger. With the helicopters and water-transport planes, fighting a fire was exactly like a combat assault in Vietnam but for the death. Long hikes were taken to reach the fires in the backcountry, and the overnight campouts in the forest were like a gift from God. Say what you may about the California penal system, but I will always be grateful for the good treatment that I received at fire camp. The experience was a good one, and the whole thing made me feel as if I was perhaps of some worth after all. The time seemed to fly by at camp, and before I knew it, my release date was upon me.

All in all, I consider my time in prison a positive experience, for when you're locked up and everything that you consider important is taken away from you, there is little to do except think. I found that thinking was very good for me, and I wondered why I hadn't done much of it in the past. There are certain things that you learn about yourself while incarcerated in a state prison. They don't come to you at first; it's not a rapid occurrence, for the first few months of prison life are filled with fear, anger, and efforts to protect yourself. It takes a while to settle in and become secure enough in you environment to give yourself the time to really open up and think hard about things. I know for a fact that prison life was harder on those around me than it was on me. St. Joseph's Orphanage and the state prison at Tracy were exactly the same except that the kids were bigger and tougher. Like at the orphanage, I found that the loudest prisoners were the weakest, the quiet ones were the ones to be watched, and it was best to lie low, stay out of trouble, and hang with a few honest and trustworthy friends—if you could find any. I found that all the things that I had considered as problems on the outside were of no importance at all, and they never were except in that little pea brain of mine that I rarely used for anything except finding dope. I found myself sinking into a deep sadness that took weeks to climb out of.

In time I found that all of these things—sadness, fear, and anger—were nothing but self-indulgence, and I was thinking of nothing but myself, my all-important self. Once I realized this fact, it became easier and easier to concentrate on things that were important to me, things that should have mattered to me all along. I found myself wanting to be a good person, an honest, trustworthy person. I also found that I had no idea how to go about it or how to prove it to others around me. I had no clue! I thought and thought about it for what seemed an eternity until I began to look around for someone who might be an honest and trustworthy person.

I looked and looked for weeks, and I found a few people who might be honest, but it wasn't until my first visit with my wife Therese that I finally found what I was looking for. When I walked into the visiting room, it hit me right in the face. How could I have been so stupid? Well, I guess that was easy for a stupid guy! There she was, standing there waiting for me with open arms, all forgiving and loving. I have to tell you that I'll never forget that moment in time, as it had such brilliance and blessed light that its imprint is burned permanently into my soul. Therese still loved me and nothing else mattered to me from that moment on, and that steadfast love that she has always given so freely to me has become all important to me. Since that moment in time, I have pondered my little mind into exhaustion trying to find ways to let her know that I love her so. It has never been an easy thing for me to show affection for others, and it was very hard for me at first. I found it extremely hard to show her how much I loved her while still in prison, and it wasn't until my release on parole that I really started to feel comfortable enough to start showing her. Once I began to open up to love, it wasn't long before I loved everybody—and I mean everybody.

Therese's family has always been very loving and affectionate toward me, but it wasn't until I realized how much I loved them that I really discovered how much love could be spread around so freely within a family. The Burton family is in a league of its own. It can only be described as totally whacko. Never in my life have I come across such a close-knit family. I have only my high-school days for any comparison, but I truly have never run across so much family togetherness and love. I certainly cannot compare the Burtons to my family, for we are a total mess. I found them all to be honest and trustworthy people and probably the only positive group of people in my entire life. I found myself realizing how important they all were to me, and I became so grateful for the love that was given to me so freely. I wish only one thing when it comes to the Paluska and the Burton famlies: that I will have the chance to show them all how much I really love them. I don't know how to go about it at this moment, but I'm working on it, and sooner or later they will know. They will know that I love them all.

With my newfound thinking skills, my mind began to go places that it had never been. All my life I have wandered to and fro, just reacting to my environment and never thinking my way through. I am totally surprised that I made it this far in life without someone beating me to death. I began traveling back in time, opening my mind to the truth of what had occurred in my past. Soon it became so easy for me to escape into deep thought that everyone around me accused me of going into a trance, and they often told me to wake up and do my time in prison like everyone else. Eventually, to escape interference, I would open a book and everyone would think that I was reading. I went back to my earliest memories, and even though it was not clear to me what had occurred, I began to consider what my father must have felt and what could possibly make him want to hurt his son. I realized that he was a sick man, and he had no idea what he had done. He, like me, was a product of his environment, and I now knew that there was no malice toward me. His actions, no matter how violent, had nothing to do with the love that he must have felt for me. This realization has helped me tremendously with my own anger and sadness that was forced upon me through my military experiences.

While I was in prison, I often found myself in situations that were exactly like the ones I experienced as a kid in the orphanage. In fact they were so similar, with the exception of the chapel that I sometimes felt as if I were back in Little Rock at St. Joseph's and I kept expecting to see Sister Conchada come around the corner with an enema bottle in her hand. I am filled with anger when I think of her and what she did to me, but at the time it was happening to me, I was so in love with her. I thought that she was so beautiful with her long black dress, and she made me feel so good. So good in fact that I would purposely get into trouble just so I could go and see her. When I think of her now, I think that she must have been a very disturbed woman, and I cannot help but think that some of the other sisters must have known what she was doing to so many of the young boys in her charge. I can't help but think of how many boys she molested during her many long years at St.

Joseph's. I thank my lucky stars that I was placed on a minimum-security yard at Jamestown State Prison. If I had been placed on a three or four yard, along with the men facing many years of incarceration, I would have had to fight to keep from being molested by the hardened criminals there. The one and two yards are like the country club prisons that you often read about, with tennis courts, basketball courts, and some organized sporting events. Of course there was a certain amount of violence, even on these minimum-security yards; after all, it is still a prison, but so was the orphanage. It too was a prison, but for children, with nuns instead of guards.

I found myself going over and over the events that I experienced while serving in the Republic of Vietnam. Therese had written and asked me to try to open up to her and tell her of all the dark, secret things that I seemed to be keeping deep inside myself. She knew that there was something bothering me, and she often tried to pry it out, to no avail. I thought it over for some time before I did tell her, in a letter, of some of the dark demons that I kept locked inside. It was not an easy thing for me to do, but I told her that I had killed a man in a field of tall grass, and that I thought that it was murder. I told her of the fact that the man was not a soldier but a farmer, a dirt-poor farmer who just happened to be in the wrong place at the wrong time. I told her how I felt like a coward because I ran away from the rest of the men on my crew just to save my own skin, the skin that I would come to consider as worthless. I told her how I wished that I could change things, but that I couldn't and that I would gladly die myself if it would bring him back. It was the first time in all these years that I had ever told anyone about that day, and it took me a week to finally drop the letter into the mailbox.

All of these bad experiences are behind me now, and I am being treated as an outpatient at a Veterans Administration mental health clinic, where it seems that now everyone in the world knows everything about me. There, I have met a woman who has a knack for making me blab about everything in the world that seems to be bothering me at the moment. She assures me that I will get better and that I will feel better, and I truly believe her. She has a wonderful gift for drawing the poison from my soul, and I know now that someone can help me through the terrible battles that I still wage within myself. I am so thankful for her help, and I am slowly but surely trying to forgive myself for my terrible crimes that were done in the name of freedom and democracy.

I have been so angry for so many years at just about everything. I have lost all faith in everything that I once cherished so dearly. I lost faith in my country, my government, and even my family. One way or another, all of them had a hand in ruining my life and destroyed everything that I loved, all the way back to my early childhood. It is only now that I can begin to heal and forgive, and I am finally learning how to love again. There is a whole new world for me out there, and I'm anxious to begin anew. I am trying to rebuild my devastated family that has scattered from one end of the United States to the other. I am searching for my lost brothers, and I pray that someday we will become a normal family. I am at the beginning of my new adventure, and for the first time, I go with a smile on my face and with love in my heart.

Donald 1970 Phu Heip Republic of Vietnam

Mike Sanders Republic of Vietnam 1969

LAST NAME - FIRST NAME - MIDDLE INITIAL	ARMY SERIAL NO.	GRADE	ARM OR SERVICE	COMPONENT
Sanders Elvin E	7 002 720	Pvt	Inf	AA

ORGANIZATION	DATE OF SEPARATION	PLACE OF SEPARATION
Company A 103rd Infantry Trg Bn	22 Jan 46	Separation Center Ft McPherson, Ga

PERMANENT ADDRESS FOR MAILING PURPOSES	DATE OF BIRTH	PLACE OF BIRTH
201 Miller St Cookeville Tenn	14 May 21	Rutherford Co Tenn

COLOR EYES	COLOR HAIR	HEIGHT	WEIGHT
Blue	Brown	5-8	130

Prosser Road T-EO.301

MILITARY HISTORY

DATE OF INDUCTION	DATE OF ENLISTMENT	PLACE OF ENTRY INTO SERVICE
13 Apr 40	13 Apr 40	Atlanta Ga

Pearl Harbor   New Guinea

DECORATIONS AND CITATIONS
American Defense Service Ribbon
Asiatic Pacific Theater Ribbon with 2 Bronze Stars
American Theater Ribbon with 1 Bronze Star

WOUNDS RECEIVED IN ACTION
None

LATEST IMMUNIZATION DATES			SERVICE OUTSIDE CONTINENTAL U.S. AND RETURN		
2 Jul 42	4 Jul 40	8 Jul 40	1 Jul 40	Hawaii	26 Jul 40
			15 Oct 44	U S	1 Nov 44

None

Convenience of Government AR 615-365 15 Dec 44 RR1-1 (Demobilization)

PAY DATA

JACK GOLDSMITH 1st Lt

INSURANCE NOTICE

Lapel Button Issued
Last 30 days under AW 107

Edwin E Sanders

TREASURY DEPARTMENT
BUREAU OF WAR RISK INSURANCE

AWARD OF COMPENSATION

To: Mr. Eadie Anthony Sanders   C-494227
Gen. Del.,
Prichard, Alabama.

In accordance with the Act of Congress of October 6, 1917, and the amend-

ments thereto, you are hereby notified that as a Pvt. 1/c Co. K, 36th Inf.

who was discharged from the   military   service of the United States on the

31st   day of   March   19 20, you are awarded compensation in the amount

of   eight and 00/100   dollars per month, from the   1st   day

of   April   19 20 on account of disability resulting from injury incurred

in the line of duty while employed in the active service.   The monthly payments
pursuant to this award shall continue during the period in which you are partially
disabled.

IMPORTANT PROVISION OF THE ACT.

"Sec. 28.—That the allotments and family allowances, compensation, and insurance payable under Articles II, III, and IV, respectively, shall not be assignable; shall not be subject to the claims of creditors of any person to whom an award is made under Article II, III, and IV, and shall be exempt from all taxation: Provided, That such allotments and family allowances, compensation, and insurance shall be subject to any claims which the United States may have, under Articles II, III, and IV, against the person on whose account the allotments and family allowances, compensation, or insurance is payable."

You are not entitled to this award nor to the payment of compensation from the Bureau of War Risk Insurance while you are in training with and receiving payments from the Federal Board for Vocational Education. If you are receiving vocational training and payments from the Federal Board for Vocational Education you should return any checks issued to you covering a period subsequent to the date of the commencement of your course of training in accordance with this award to the Compensation and Claims Division, Bureau of War Risk Insurance, Washington, D. C., with a statement showing the date you started training. From the date that you begin vocational training you will be paid by the Federal Board for Vocational Education.

You are required to make a monthly report stating as near as possible your exact physical condition, together with all information relative to your return to employment or increase in earning capacity. Failure to make such monthly report will terminate your compensation payments until such report is received.

The initial payment check pursuant to the award approved in your favor will be dispatched to you at the earliest possible moment. If you should change your present address, the Compensation and Claims Division, Bureau of War Risk Insurance, Washington, D. C., must be immediately notified. All future communications with reference to this case must bear the Compensation Number C   494227

Authorized by the Bureau of War Risk Insurance this 2nd day of   November   , 1920.

E. H. HARPER
Assistant Director,
In Charge of Compensation Claims Div.

Per   A. C. D.

ABOUT THE AUTHOR

Donald K. Sanders is a columnist for the *Winters Express* newspaper of Winters, California, where he lives. He also has a column at the iPinion Syndicate web page for award-winning and talented columnist. He is a disabled Vietnam veteran and is retired.

The Death of My Inner Self

By Donald K. Sanders

I think that my "inner being" is dying. It no longer communicates with me. When this first occurred I found that it meant big trouble for my physical, outer being. It seems that the two are connected; interlaced like a vine through a tree.

For simplification, I will hereon refer to them as my "innie" and "outie." Our "innie" is our only link to the great cosmos, if you will, or the great lake of super intelligence from whence you may sip tidbits of information that quench the thirst of your very soul. Our "innie" is not of this Earth. It is a gift from God to give us direction; the right from wrong thingy.

Some 40 years ago I experienced a traumatic event that my "innie" could not handle. I began getting "error" messages from my "innie" forcing my "outie" to fend for itself in a war zone. I had been in Vietnam for over a year and a half when my "outie" decided that we didn't need my "innie" because therein lies internal pain and sorrow.

"We can survive on our own" it said, "we don't need that stuff".

As it turned out, if you don't listen to and use your "innie" it slows down, gets sick, and eventually dies. So here is the whole ball of wax. The truth is that if your "innie" is sick or dying, you can bet that it is just a matter of time before your "outie" follows suit. Your "outie" belongs to the physical world, so when it becomes sick, others will notice your lack of direction and focus. What is right and what is wrong is no longer clear, so a slow but ever-growing distance begins to separate you from everything that you need to lead a happy and productive life.

Since that terrible day in 1971, my "outie" has been searching everywhere for information about how I may nourish and sooth my troubled soul. Unfortunately, the "outie" is restricted to the physical world. Here, nothing is to be found but logic and science; both of which have caused immeasurable horror, suffering, and sadness to the universe. War, famine, disease, and all other unimaginable evil things that occur in our physical world are a direct result of science and logic.

Like so many other men of yesterday and today, who find themselves in a war zone unable to find nourishment for their soul in the physical world, I turned inward but there I found the "error" message. It seems that your "innie" has trouble interpreting warfare.

Nothing of value can be found anywhere in any war; absolutely nothing. Your "innie" will scream as loudly as it possibly can, "Wait, stop, don't do that, please, please!" Of course your "outie" cannot comply or you become a statistic of war. Thus the conflict between inside and outside begins. and as many have found, the conflict between the two is continuous and will never end. "Error, error, error," is all that you will receive from your "innie" for all of eternity.

I have seen hundreds of doctors and taken thousands of pills. I have talked with 50 or so psychiatrists and I have come to the conclusion that none of this can help my "innie." I have accepted this as a simple fact of truth. The thing that I cannot accept is the fact that we are still sending our children to worthless, no-account, bastard wars where they too will lose their "innie." We will pack away our sons and daughters, without question, without reason, and send them to slaughter or be slaughtered. The very moment that we agree to send them to a needless war, we become our own worst enemy. We do not need someone to kill our children. We are doing it ourselves.

Taking the life of another human being and watching the life blood flow from his body will, in a single moment, tear your soul apart. It cannot be fixed by doctors or pills and it will never go away. You cannot go back and do things in a different way. There is no second chance.

It is horrible, the act of killing; it sends an evil ripple backwards through time and space to your earliest ancestor and forward to your unborn descendants. The ripple affects everything the killer and his victim has ever been conscious of. It takes everything away forever and gives you nothing in return.

There are two things that I would hope to be true. First, I would like our new president to be a man of peace. The second thing is a requirement of the first. A man of peace must have a healthy "innie."

May 27, 2010 iPinion Syndicate,

May 2010 Winters Express, Winters California

Made in the USA
San Bernardino, CA
04 October 2015